# SUPER BUCS

## TAMPA BAY'S RISE TO SUPER BOWL CHAMPIONS

## Orlando Sentinel

OrlandoSentinel.com

www.sportspublishingllc.com

**PUBLISHER**
Peter L. Bannon

**SENIOR MANAGING EDITORS**
Susan M. Moyer and
Joseph J. Bannon, Jr.

**COORDINATING EDITOR**
Noah Adams Amstadter

**DEVELOPMENTAL EDITORS**
Mark E. Zulauf, Gabe A. Rosen and
Erin Linden-Levy

**ART DIRECTOR**
K. Jeffrey Higgerson

**BOOK DESIGN**
Jennifer L. Polson

**COVER DESIGN**
Kenneth J. O'Brien and Joseph Brumleve

**BOOK LAYOUT**
Jennifer L. Polson and Tracy Gaudreau

**IMAGING**
Christine Mohrbacher, Kenneth J. O'Brien,
Kerri Baker and Joseph Brumleve

**COPY EDITOR**
Cynthia L. McNew

# Orlando Sentinel

OrlandoSentinel.com

**PRESIDENT AND PUBLISHER**
Kathleen M. Waltz

**EDITOR AND VICE PRESIDENT**
Tim Franklin

**MANAGING EDITOR**
Elaine Kramer

**ASSOCIATE MANAGING EDITOR/SPORTS**
Van McKenzie

**ASSOCIATE MANAGING EDITOR/
PRESENTATION**
Monty Cook

**ASSOCIATE MANAGING EDITOR/
CONTENT DEVELOPMENT**
Steve Doyle

**EDITORIAL SYSTEMS SUPPORT MANAGER**
George Remaine

**SENIOR SYSTEMS SUPPORT MANAGER**
Bob Glasgow

**SENIOR ARCHIVES SPECIALIST**
Judy Alderman

**TRIBUNE SPORTS COORDINATOR**
John Cherwa

© 2003 Orlando Sentinel
All Rights Reserved.

No part of this book may be reproduced in any form or by any electronic or
mechanical means including information storage and retrieval systems —
except in the case of brief quotations embodied in critical articles or reviews —
without permission in writing from its publisher, Sports Publishing L.L.C.
All stories and photographs are from the files of the *Orlando Sentinel.*

Front and Back Cover Photos: Shoun A. Hill/Orlando Sentinel

ISBN: 1-58261-701-5

# EDITOR'S NOTE

To those who have followed the Tampa Bay Buccaneers from their 26-loss beginning, through miserly maneuverings, downright dumb decisions and double-digit-loss seasons, this story must not seem possible.

The Tampa Bay Buccaneers have won Super Bowl XXXVII in San Diego.

Punchlines to more jokes than maybe any football team in history, the Bucs are now at the pinnacle.

Can these be the same Bucs as those who went almost two full seasons before winning a game?

Are these the Bucs whose first coach, John McKay, when asked about his team's execution, said, "I'm all for it"?

Is this the franchise whose tight-fisted owner, Hugh Culverhouse, let eventual Super Bowl MVP quarterback Doug Williams walk to the United States Football League when the Bucs were a playoff team?

Is this the team that lost nearly three out of every four games for more than 20 years?

Is this the team that had never won a game when the temperature at kickoff was below 40 degrees?

Are these the old, orange-and-white-clad "Yucs," whose fans wore bags over their heads?

No, these are the Tampa Bay Buccaneers, snarling pirates in pewter and red.

They are a talent-laden band assembled by General Manager Rich McKay, John's son, and developed by Coach Tony Dungy, a defensive whiz who arrived in 1996 and transformed them into contenders in just three seasons.

It's the franchise whose owners, Malcolm Glazer and his sons, fired Dungy in early 2002 and spent $8 million and four draft choices to acquire Jon Gruden, the coach of the Oakland Raiders.

It's the team that Gruden in one season polished to a Super Bowl shine.

This is the story of Gruden's season, a tale that starts with frustration in September at home, where the Bucs lost an overtime opener New Orleans when their punter's pass was intercepted in his end zone.

It weaves through narrow victories carved by powerful defense against Baltimore, Cincinnati and Carolina.

It includes the steady improvement of an offense led by quarterback Brad Johnson and greater support for the heroics of Derrick Brooks, Warren Sapp, John Lynch, Simeon Rice and Ronde Barber.

It flows from a frustrating, pre-Christmas loss to Pittsburgh on Monday Night Football, when Johnson was injured, to a postseason of dominance.

The Bucs overpowered the San Francisco 49ers to open the playoffs and then went to Philadelphia—where their last two playoff bids had ended on frigid nights before derisive fans—and on an icy January afternoon throttled the Eagles and their throng, 27-10.

That Gruden and the Bucs would face his old team, the Raiders, in the Super Bowl was beyond most of our imaginations. The author of this book might have been Mother Goose, so fantastic is its finish.

But the writers, photographers and editors at the Orlando Sentinel were the chroniclers, and we offer you their stories of how this dramatic tale meandered from training camp at Disney World to its fabulous finish in San Diego. We were there every day and have all the storylines.

We think you'll find that it's a season worth reliving.

*Tim Franklin*

**Tim Franklin**

## Gruden excited to be with Bucs

Mike Holmgren predicted great things for Jon Gruden and using a driver who he doubted was old enough to have a license. He was right, and Gruden was in Green Bay.

Gruden is just dying to dig Bucs out of hole

## Miami survives a nail-biter

9th time may be the charm for Dolphins

## Jacksonville makes plays in clutch

## Head games give Coughlin winning edge

# Sports

Dolphins look good    Rose draws big crowd

## Bucs keep grasp over lost Rams

You never know what to expect from the NFL

Tampa Bay had Kurt Warner pressured and confused in a 26-14 home victory.

# NECESSARY ROUGHNESS!

# State of the NFL

That's National Florida League for 1st-place Bucs, Dolphins and Ja

# Game Day

Ratings game    Monday Night Football    More Sports, Section C

# Flattened in Philly

QB Lucas struggles in his 1st start

Offense fails to reach end zone; Bucs lose 4th straight to Eagles

# Game Day

Playing Favre-ites    A Giant pain    More sports, Section C

## NFL's lone star

The Cowboys' Emmitt Smith breaks the all-time rushing mark

Emmitt tops when it comes to size of heart

# Whew!

Jags beaten, kicked around

Jag's offense can't deliver when needed

Super Bowl champs fall again

# Game Day

Mare hits game-winner for Dolphins

Most valuable Buc? Not who you think it is

## George has 113 yards to lift Titans

# Chuggin' along

Bucs win their 5th in a row

# Game Day

Packers tripped by Vikes    Monday Night Football    More sports, Section C

# In the zone

Bucs are proof there are a lot of ways to win

It's open season on star QBs

# Game Day

Dolphins tonight    Jags' heartbreaker    Pats, Jets win

Tampa Bay Buccaneers 34, Atlanta Falcons 10

# Back on track

Bucs prove that Vick can't do it all — after all

Vick's highlights spice Falcons' win

# Game Day

NFL turkeys cooked    Dolphins face Favre & his pack    Magic's Hill to play

# Happy Days

Violent hits take unseen toll on both sides of ball

**On a roll**

# CRUNCH TIME

# Orlando Sentinel

**'Chicago,' 'The Hours' win big** | **McGrady scores 35 as Magic beat Raptors 101-95** | **Universal, SeaWorld take aim at Disney's supremacy**

---

**NFC Championship** | **AFC Championship**

# Bucs don't stop here!

### Tampa Bay crushes San Francisco to reach NFC title game

---

## Game consumes Gruden, most great coaches

# Super Deal

Desperately seeking a high-impact coach, the Bucs paid dearly but got the right man.

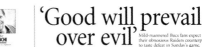

---

# BUCS BOWL-BOUND

### TEAM BURIES EAGLES — AND ITS PAST — 27-10

Oakland Raiders beat Tennessee Titans 41-24 to claim AFC Championship

Gruden looks forward to meeting his old team with Super Bowl title on the line

LOOK FOR A SPECIAL SUPER BOWL XXXVII SECTION INSIDE TODAY AND EVERY DAY

**Give up power, U.S. tells Saddam**

---

### SUPER BOWL XXXVII SPECIAL
# Orlando Sentinel

## LEGEND OF THE ROCK

## Secret uncovered

This Bucs traveling super show stars the Rock

## Jurevicius arrives ready for Raiders

With his newborn son's health improving, the Bucs' wide receiver can concentrate on the Super Bowl.

**Old man Romo keeps rollin' along**

---

### SUPER BOWL SPECIAL SECTION
# Super Bowl

SUNDAY, 6:18 P.M. | BUCS VS. RAIDERS | ABC, WFTV-CH. 9

# 'Good will' prevail over evil'

Mild-mannered Bucs fans expect their obnoxious Raiders counterparts to taste defeat in Sunday's game.

### Johnson won't talk? That'll be the day

---

### SUPER BOWL XXXVII SPECIAL
# Orlando Sentinel

# CHUCKY VS. BLAND BILL

Call him what you want, Gruden protégé Callahan is quietly going about making a name for himself.

**Marvelous Rice is ageless wonder**

## Glazers have shepherded Bucs' rise from the ashes

---

### 12-PAGE SOUVENIR CHAMPIONSHIP EDITION INSIDE
# Orlando Sentinel

# MEGA-BUCS!

### TAMPA BAY DOMINATES OAKLAND 48-21 FOR 1ST SUPER BOWL TITLE

**DEVASTATING DEFENSE:** Bucs defenders picked off Raiders quarterback Rich Gannon 5 times

**JUST LOSE, BABY:** Tampa Bay's big investment paid off as coach Jon Gruden mastered his former team

**Bucs' victory after 27 years of trying whips Tampa Bay fans into frenzy**

---

### SOUVENIR EDITION
# Super Bowl

# CHAMPS!

### Almighty Bucs repel the Raiders 48-21 as Gruden leads Tampa Bay to 1st NFL title

## Supercalifragilisticexpialidocious!

# BUCS SPORT NEW LOOK

## BY CHRIS HARRY, ORLANDO SENTINEL

During Saturday's joint workouts against Miami, Michael Pittman zipped out of the backfield and ran an out-and-up on Dolphins linebacker Scott Galyon. Tampa Bay's new starting tailback sped past Galyon, down the sideline and hauled in a perfect throw from backup quarterback Rob Johnson for a 40-yard touchdown.

As Pittman crossed the goal line to applause from the crowd, he flexed his arms and torso.

"I was pumped up," Pittman said. "And I'll be even more pumped up if I catch one in a game."

His first chance will come tonight when the Bucs and the Dolphins open their preseason schedule with a nationally televised game at Raymond James Stadium.

If Pittman is going to score, however, he'd better do it quickly. While tonight may mark the game debut of new coach Jon Gruden and his reworked offense, the starters are not expected to play for more than a series or two.

In other words, a warehouse of inventory will be on hand, but only a closetful will be on display.

"We want to come together as a football team, obviously," Gruden said following Sunday's abbreviated practice of mostly special teams at Disney's Wide World of Sports. "We want to play well, we want to execute and we want to play a physical football game. We want to win. At the same time, we want to play a lot of guys."

So if the 65,000-plus fans are coming to get a close look at the six new starters on

BELOW: Buccaneers head coach Jon Gruden addresses the media during his first press conference in Tampa. Chris Livingston/Orlando Sentinel

RIGHT: Buccaneers head coach Jon Gruden speaks with receiver Keyshawn Johnson at Tampa Bay's training camp at Disney's Wide World of Sports. John Raoux/Orlando Sentinel

**ABOVE:** Warren Sapp exits the field quickly after a July 29 practice, leaving waiting fans at Disney's Wide World of Sports no chance for an autograph.

John Raoux/Orlando Sentinel

offense, they won't be sticking around long. Instead, they'll have to settle for getting an idea of what Gruden's system will look like in action, how it will attack and how it will finish drives.

Even some players are eager to know.

"I'll be a fan, but I'll keep my opinion to myself because they're still learning," linebacker Derrick Brooks said of the guys on the other side of the ball. "Each day you see them getting more comfortable. You see the receivers having better communication with the quarterback. You see it coming."

Starting quarterback Brad Johnson will work a dozen or so plays before giving way to Rob Johnson and Shaun King. The team's most notable free-agent acquisitions—Pittman, wide receiver Keenan McCardell, tight end Ken Dilger and offensive lineman Kerry Jenkins—likely will bail early with the rest of the first-team offense.

A notable exception could be at the tackle positions, where Roman Oben has replaced second-year pro Kenyatta Walker on the left side. Walker, who started 17 games there as a rookie last season, is back at right tackle, where he excelled for three seasons at Florida. He can expect some extra reps in his first game since flip-flopping sides.

But rookies such as tailback Travis Stephens, the former Tennessee standout taken in the fourth round,

along with wide receiver Aaron Locker, linebacker Ryan Nece, safety Jermaine Phillips and cornerback Tim Wansley, will be closely scrutinized. Of the new veterans, tight end Marco Battaglia and wideout E. G. Green could see a little extended action in working with Rob Johnson and King.

"We have 87 or 88 guys on this team," Gruden said. "There's a good chance they're all going to play."

Ditto the Dolphins. Don't expect heavy doses of Ricky Williams in his Miami debut.

"Let's not kid ourselves, we're going to see different plays and different things than what we've seen out here in practice," said Dolphins coach Dave Wannstedt, whose team must turn around and play its second game Thursday against New Orleans. "But what I'm excited about is, without a game plan, you're just lining up and seeing how guys adjust to football situations."

It is, after all, only a preseason game—the first of four.

Some may view it as Gruden's grand intro to Tampa Bay. The coach does not. In fact, he remembers his first home preseason game as a head coach. It was August 1998 at Oakland and Tampa Bay came to town.

The Bucs won 41-7.

"Hopefully, it'll be a heckuva lot better than that one," he said.

> **"We have 87 or 88 guys on this team. There's a good chance they're all going to play."**
>
> — Bucs head coach Jon Gruden

**ABOVE:** Tampa Bay's Ronde Barber drags Miami ball carrier Chris Chambers out of bounds after a short reception during an August 12 preseason game. John Raoux/Orlando Sentinel

## NEW ORLEANS 26

### GAME ONE

## TAMPA BAY 20

# THE BAD-NEWS BUCS

### BY CHRIS HARRY, ORLANDO SENTINEL

The dawn of the Jon Gruden era will be remembered for the error—and as one of the most bizarre losses in Tampa Bay Buccaneers history.

New Orleans running back Fred McAfee ripped through the Bucs' punt protection, swarmed punter Tom Tupa in the end zone and forced him into a pass that was as desperate as it was despicable.

Tupa's throw had no chance of finding any receiver other than Saints linebacker James Allen, who gladly cradled the ball from point-blank range for an interception and touchdown to give the Saints a 26-20 overtime victory Sunday in front of a silenced Raymond James Stadium crowd of 65,554.

The defeat spoiled an admirable comeback by the Bucs in their first game under Gruden, who held his team together despite terrible play from its offensive line and defense.

"I'm disappointed, but I'm not going to be the one to let this fester for very long," Gruden said. "We have a good football team and we're going to come back from this."

The Bucs (0-1) came back from an awful first half, falling behind 13-3 after being outgained by the Saints (1-0) 203-77 in total yards.

The teams traded touchdowns in the third quarter, as New Orleans quarterback Aaron Brooks cancelled out a Brad Johnson-to-Keenan McCardell score of four yards by hitting rookie wideout Donte Stallworth for a 41-yard touchdown strike and 20-10 lead.

There it stood with just under three minutes to play, until Johnson led the offense to 10 points in the final 2:41. Martin Gramatica nailed a 40-yard field goal as time expired to force overtime.

Tampa Bay had three chances in OT; the last was a three and out that set up the zany finish.

"If you are in the league long enough, you will see everything," Saints coach Jim Haslett said. "I can't remember anything like this, and I've been in some crazy games."

**OPPOSITE:** Bucs defensive end Greg Spires is all over Saints quarterback Aaron Brooks in the fourth quarter. The Bucs' defense held the Saints scoreless in the fourth quarter, while the Tampa Bay offense put 10 points on the board, sending the game to overtime.
Gary W. Green/ Orlando Sentinel

**ABOVE:** Bucs coach Jon Gruden and quarterback Brad Johnson watch with disappointment from the sideline during the fourth quarter. Gary W. Green/Orlando Sentinel

**OPPOSITE:** Bucs punter Tom Tupa feels the heat from Saints defender Fred McAfee in overtime. Tupa then pulled the ball down and attempted a desperation pass that was intercepted by Saints linebacker James Allen and returned for the game-winning touchdown. Gary W. Green/Orlando Sentinel

| | 1st | 2nd | 3rd | 4th | OT | Final |
|---|---|---|---|---|---|---|
| New Orleans | 6 | 7 | 7 | 0 | 6 | 26 |
| Tampa Bay | 0 | 3 | 7 | 10 | 0 | 20 |

## SCORING SUMMARY

| Qtr | Team | Play | | Time |
|---|---|---|---|---|
| 1st | Saints | FG | Carney 28-yd. field goal | 8:18 |
| 1st | Saints | FG | Carney 41-yd. field goal | 0:24 |
| 2nd | Buccaneers | FG | Gramatica 52-yd. field goal | 13:24 |
| 2nd | Saints | TD | Williams 32-yd. pass from Brooks (Carney kick) | 4:17 |
| 3rd | Buccaneers | TD | McCardell 4-yd. pass from B. Johnson (Gramatica kick) | 11:39 |
| 3rd | Saints | TD | Stallworth 41-yd. pass from Brooks | 8:46 |
| 4th | Buccaneers | TD | Jurevicius 11-yd. pass from B. Johnson (Gramatica kick) | 2:47 |
| 4th | Buccaneers | FG | Gramatica 40-yd. field goal | 0:04 |
| OT | Saints | TD | Allen 0-yd. interception return | 2:59 |

## OFFENSE

### SAINTS

| PASSING | COMP | ATT | YDS | TD | INT |
|---|---|---|---|---|---|
| Brooks | 24 | 42 | 260 | 2 | 1 |

| RECEIVING | REC | YDS | TD |
|---|---|---|---|
| Horn | 8 | 108 | 0 |
| Stallworth | 4 | 63 | 1 |
| Williams | 1 | 32 | 1 |
| Pathon | 2 | 15 | 0 |
| McAllister | 4 | 12 | 0 |
| Reed | 1 | 12 | 0 |
| Sloan | 1 | 12 | 0 |
| Smith | 3 | 6 | 0 |

| RUSHING | ATT | YDS | TD |
|---|---|---|---|
| McAllister | 31 | 109 | 0 |
| Brooks | 3 | 9 | 0 |

### BUCCANEERS

| PASSING | COMP | ATT | YDS | TD | INT |
|---|---|---|---|---|---|
| B. Johnson | 28 | 52 | 278 | 2 | 0 |
| Tupa | 0 | 1 | 0 | 0 | 1 |

| RECEIVING | REC | YDS | TD |
|---|---|---|---|
| K. Johnson | 5 | 76 | 0 |
| McCardell | 6 | 63 | 1 |
| Alstott | 4 | 48 | 0 |
| Jurevicius | 4 | 37 | 1 |
| Pittman | 5 | 31 | 0 |
| Yoder | 1 | 10 | 0 |
| Dilger | 2 | 7 | 0 |
| Stephens | 1 | 6 | 0 |

| RUSHING | ATT | YDS | TD |
|---|---|---|---|
| Pittman | 12 | 50 | 0 |
| Alstott | 6 | 11 | 0 |
| B. Johnson | 3 | 11 | 0 |

**ABOVE: Bucs receiver Keyshawn Johnson is slow to get up after missing a pass in the third quarter.** Gary W. Green/Orlando Sentinel

## TAMPA BAY 25
### GAME TWO
## BALTIMORE 0

# BUCS DINE ON STUFFED BIRDS

**BY CHRIS HARRY, ORLANDO SENTINEL**

The Tampa Bay Buccaneers can only wonder what the all-around effort they put forth Sunday might have meant last week against New Orleans.

For now, they'll gladly accept that it was enough to drop a goose egg in a Ravens' nest.

The Bucs couldn't find the end zone on offense, but managed to score from everywhere else in a 25-0 win over the Baltimore Ravens that gave coach Jon Gruden his first victory in pewter and red in front of a fast-exiting crowd of 69,304 at Ravens Stadium.

Karl Williams returned a punt 56 yards for a touchdown, Martin Gramatica kicked three field goals, and the Tampa Bay defense scored on a safety and 97-yard interception return by Derrick Brooks that iced the fifth shutout in franchise history.

"There's not a lot of time in the NFL to be sentimental when you got the [0-2] St. Louis Rams waiting on you," said Gruden, who awarded game balls to every member of the team. "I thought we took command early and stayed in command."

Quarterback Brad Johnson was 24 of 31 for 211 yards, with all but 55 coming in the first half as the Bucs (1-1) built a 13-0 halftime lead. The offense that was supposed to be much improved this season failed to reach the end zone, but controlled the clock for 31 of the first 45 minutes.

"A pretty thorough whipping in every phase," said Baltimore coach Brian Billick, whose roster has 19 rookies and 10 players who made the first start of their careers just a week ago.

That begs this question: what did this victory tell us about the Bucs? The offense failed to make it into the end zone. The defense that needed three quarters to find its groove a week ago dominated, but it was going against inexperienced quarterback Chris Redman (16 of 38, 141 yards, one interception) and the rebuilt Ravens, who finished with 173 total yards.

"Shutouts are very hard to come by, but it takes a team effort," strong safety John Lynch said. "We played outstanding defense, but the offense controlled the clock in the first half. Then the special teams pitched in."

It makes you wonder where these Bucs were a week ago.

"[The Saints] came out last week and attacked; we just could never counter," said cornerback Ronde Barber, who had five tackles and six pass breakups. "We got hit with a right and near knocked out in the first round. But we buckled up and showed some people what we're about today."

**ABOVE: Dwight Smith of the Bucs looks on as kick returner Karl Williams dives into the end zone after returning a punt 56 yards for a touchdown against the Ravens in the first quarter. The play put the Bucs up 10-0 in the game, a lead they did not give up.**
Roberto Borea, AP/Wide World Photos

Sunday was the Bucs' fifth shutout in the franchise's 27-season history:

| Year | Opponent | Score | The buzz |
|------|----------|-------|----------|
| 1979 | Kansas City | 3-0 | Bucs clinch first division title in downpour. |
| 1985 | St. Louis | 16-0 | Steve Young debuts with a victory for the 0-9 Bucs. |
| 1998 | at Cincinnati | 35-0 | Final game, eliminated from playoffs on flight home. |
| 2000 | Chicago | 41-0 | Maybe most dominating performance in team history. |
| 2002 | at Baltimore | 25-0 | A shutout with no offensive touchdowns. |

**" A pretty thorough whipping in every phase."**

**— Baltimore coach Brian Billick**

**ABOVE: Bucs defensive tackle Warren Sapp body-slams Ravens running back Chester Taylor to the ground in the first quarter. The hit drew a penalty, but the Ravens didn't capitalize and were shut out by the Bucs' defense the rest of the way.** Roberto Borea, AP/Wide World Photos

**RIGHT: Ravens safety Ed Reed looks on as Bucs receiver Keyshawn Johnson hauls in a pass for a 20-yard gain during the first quarter.** Nick Wass. AP/Wide World Photos

| | 1st | 2nd | 3rd | 4th | Final |
|---|---|---|---|---|---|
| Tampa Bay | 10 | 3 | 5 | 7 | 25 |
| Baltimore | 0 | 0 | 0 | 0 | 0 |

## SCORING SUMMARY

| Qtr | Team | Play | .................................................... | Time |
|---|---|---|---|---|
| 1st | Buccaneers | FG | Gramatica 36-yd. field goal ................................................ | 7:50 |
| 1st | Buccaneers | TD | Williams 56-yd. punt return (Gramatica kick) ...................... | 2:13 |
| 2nd | Buccaneers | FG | Gramatica 30-yd. field goal ................................................ | 3:57 |
| 3rd | Buccaneers | SFT | Safety ................................................................................ | 14:54 |
| 3rd | Buccaneers | FG | Gramatica 30-yd. field goal ................................................ | 8:30 |
| 4th | Buccaneers | TD | Brooks 97-yd. interception return (Gramatica kick) .................... | |

## OFFENSE

### BUCCANEERS

| COMP | ATT | YDS | TD | INT |
|---|---|---|---|---|
| B. Johnson | 24 | 31 | 211 | 0 | 0 |

| RECEIVING | REC | YDS | TD |
|---|---|---|---|
| Pittman | 6 | 58 | 0 |
| K. Johnson | 3 | 47 | 0 |
| McCardell | 4 | 38 | 0 |
| Alstott | 5 | 25 | 0 |
| Jurevicius | 2 | 18 | 0 |
| Cook | 1 | 14 | 0 |
| Stecker | 3 | 11 | |

| RUSHING | ATT | YDS | TD |
|---|---|---|---|
| Pittman | 13 | 37 | 0 |
| Alstott | 11 | 23 | 0 |
| Stecker | 5 | 15 | 0 |
| B. Johnson | 1 | -1 | 0 |

### RAVENS

| PASSING | COMP | ATT | YDS | TD | INT |
|---|---|---|---|---|---|
| Redman | 16 | 38 | 141 | 0 | 1 |

| RECEIVING | REC | YDS | TD |
|---|---|---|---|
| Stokley | 4 | 57 | 0 |
| Lewis | 5 | 38 | 0 |
| Heap | 3 | 20 | 0 |
| Taylor | 2 | 18 | 0 |
| Jones | 1 | 7 | 0 |
| Ricard | 1 | 1 | 0 |

| RUSHING | ATT | YDS | TD |
|---|---|---|---|
| Lewis | 17 | 53 | 0 |
| Taylor | 2 | 2 | 0 |
| Redman | 1 | 0 | 0 |

**ABOVE:** Ravens quarterback Chris Redman gives chase as Bucs linebacker Derrick Brooks runs back an interception for a touchdown in the fourth quarter. Roberto Borea, AP/Wide World Photos

# JON GRUDEN

## Get Ready for the Grind

DAVID WHITLEY, ORLANDO SENTINEL

It was 4:00 a.m., and there were two people at One Buc Place. The guy outside in the guard shack was there because he had to be.

So was the guy inside on the treadmill. His motto:

"Do what it takes to win," Jon Gruden said.

So he ran and lifted weights. He showered and looked at videotape. He made calls and worked the computer.

Maybe Gruden doesn't have to be at work at 4:00 a.m. But you don't win the Super Bowl by stopping to watch the sun rise. Besides, nobody needs to tell Gruden it's a new day in Tampa.

Al Davis ransomed four high draft picks and $8 million out of the Bucs, who were desperate to save face after their coaching search turned into a national sitcom. Gruden knows what people are saying.

"They gave up too much," he said.

"They gave up way too much. They gave up way, way too much."

The Bucs could have gotten Gruden for a cup of Gatorade, and he still would be in the office three hours before sunrise. Now he has one more motivating factor to do whatever it takes.

"Grinding" is how Gruden puts it.

Nobody doubts the 38-year-old boy wonder will grind. The doubt is whether anyone can finish the job Tony Dungy began.

Too few points and too much backroom bickering sidetracked Tampa Bay's rise from the NFL muck. The offense may take awhile to get going, and there may be some casualties along the way.

But you get the feeling the nonsense will immediately stop. If that brings casualties, so be it.

Ready or not, the Bucs are about to enter the Gruden Grinder. So far, everything they had heard is true.

That was obvious last week when the Bucs had a player in for a tryout. Most coaches would have stood on the sideline with the personnel guys. Gruden looked as if he was coaching the final minute of a playoff game in a New England snowstorm.

He pointed and flailed and probably ran more than the player. Tampa Bay players should be advised to read the NFL's collective bargaining agreement, specifically the section on how hard they can be pushed in the off season.

"Not to say he does anything to violate the CBA, but he stretches it a bit," general manager Rich McKay said.

"We'd better get some more arms around here, because the guys are going to be tired. And legs? They're going to be running a little bit."

All signs say the workaholism has paid off. Only to Gruden, it's never been work.

Depending on whom you ask, the Bucs were slightly out of focus last season. Or their locker room was bloated by egos and agendas.

The largest ones belong to Keyshawn Johnson and Warren Sapp. Johnson melted down following the playoff loss to Philadelphia, railing against unnamed teammates he said needed a butt-kicking.

Gruden's take:

"That's something I'm going to have to get a feel for. But I'm confident there's a good working relationship there, and something that we'll look at."

Translation: There will be harmony, or else.

Then there's the offense. Gruden's take:

"I'm really impressed with what I see from a defensive standpoint."

Translation: Watch out.

Word is Gruden looked at the Bucs' offensive personnel and came away with the opinion many fans developed. There's not much there of which to be scared.

He has all but declared Brad Johnson's quarterback position up for grabs. If that bothers Johnson, he's not letting on. If anything, he's enthused at the prospect of operating a proven offensive attack.

"It will all come down to players making plays," Johnson said.

"But they put you in position to be successful."

Which was more than you could say about Tampa Bay's old system. The contrast between Dungy and Gruden goes beyond offensive philosophies and their approach to the English language.

Nobody questioned Dungy's work ethic or dedication. He expected his players to behave like adults, however, and often gave them more rope than they deserved. Now the reins will be tightened. It's a new day in Tampa Bay, even if the man responsible is too busy to step outside most mornings to see it.

"So far, so good," Gruden said. "We're undefeated right now. It's been great and I'm very excited to have an opportunity to coach where I'm from. But I also realize that we have to get results."

Chucky has come full circle, but he knows this isn't child's play. That's why he is so organized. That's why he is so intense. That's why he never hits the snooze button.

He was born to grind, and he's determined to win.

Whatever it takes.

Gary W. Green/Orlando Sentinel

## ST LOUIS 14
### GAME THREE
## TAMPA BAY 26

# BUCS KEEP GRASP OVER LOST RAMS

**BY CHRIS HARRY, ORLANDO SENTINEL**

The Tampa Bay Buccaneers still have St. Louis's regular-season number while the once-feared and explosive Rams are searching for a number— any number— in the win column.

The punch that coach Jon Gruden was supposed to bring to the Bucs' offense hasn't shown up yet, but the defense that has defined the franchise for the past seven years was ready for prime time Monday night in a 26-14 victory before a frenzied Raymond James Stadium crowd of 65,652.

Derrick Brooks intercepted Kurt Warner and returned it 39 yards for a touchdown—with defensive tackle Warren Sapp leading the way and planting Warner into the end zone—with 59 seconds to play to put an exclamation point on a game the Bucs (2-1) desperately needed.

"I'm really proud of our players, but we got a lot of help from the 12th man," Gruden said. "The fans were great. This was an emotional win for us."

Defensive end Simeon Rice and cornerback Brian Kelly set up Bucs touchdowns with long interception returns, and Martin Gramatica added two field goals.

"This team is about defense," cornerback Ronde Barber said. "Always has been, always will be."

Added Sapp: "It's about our ability to rush with all our linemen."

Not only did the Bucs win for the second straight week, but they also hung a third straight Monday Night Football defeat on the Rams (0-3). Tampa Bay held St. Louis to two touchdowns, forced four interceptions and registered five sacks, as Warner, the top-rated passer in NFL history, once again was unable to solve the Bucs' Cover 2 defense.

The odds-on favorites in the NFC to return to the Super Bowl for the third time in four years, the Rams face the daunting task of becoming the first NFC team to start 0-3 and reach the league title game. No 0-3 team ever has won the Super Bowl.

"We have to dig ourselves out of this hole," St. Louis coach Mike Martz said. "We have to fight back."

The Rams ripped off a nine-play, 91-yard touchdown drive on their first possession to take a 7-3 lead after the Bucs had driven 60 yards on 11 plays and settled for a field goal. Marshall Faulk's five-yard touchdown run gave St. Louis an early lead and probably a false sense of security.

For the Bucs, it was a wake-up call.

"We all took a back seat and said, 'Whoa! This is the St. Louis Rams,'" Sapp said. "There was a shock to it."

Faulk, the MVP of the league two of the past three seasons, left the game in the first half with a neck strain and did not return. St. Louis's offense, it seemed, went with him.

---

**OPPOSITE: Bucs wide receiver Keenan McCardell gets by Rams cornerback Aeneas Williams.**
Scott Martin, AP/Wide World Photos

**ABOVE: Bucs cornerback Brian Kelly intercepts a pass in the third quarter against St. Louis.**
Gary W. Green/Orlando Sentinel

The Rams' next eight drives netted only 118 yards, with five ending in punts and three with interceptions. The Bucs, who failed to get to Warner on the first drive, mixed three sacks in for good measure.

With his team down 7-3, Rice's interception and 30-yard runback in the second quarter came after he dropped into coverage from his right end position on a zone blitz. Warner rifled a pass into Rice's number, and he was off and running.

The play set in motion Tampa Bay's only touchdown drive of the night—and its first in 17 possessions dating to the season opener against New Orleans. A timely 21-yard pass from Brad Johnson to Keyshawn Johnson, who made a spectacular fingertip grab down the sideline on third and 14, kept the drive alive. A nine-yard touchdown pass to tight end Rickey Dudley, signed just six days earlier, gave the Bucs the lead—for good, as it turned out.

Kelly's pick early in the fourth quarter, with a 31-yard return to St. Louis's one, set up a touchdown blast from fullback Mike Alstott, who plowed through linebacker Tommy Polley with 10 minutes, 42 seconds to go for a 19-7 lead. The attempt for a two-point conversion failed.

After better than two quarters of confusion, Warner rediscovered his rhythm midway through the fourth period, leading the Rams on an 11-play drive that ended on a fourth-and-one play with third-team tailback Lamar Gordon taking a toss to the right, hitting a seam and high-stepping for a 21-yard run that drew St. Louis to 19-14 with 4:21 to play.

The Rams then held the Bucs on downs and forced a punt. Tom Tupa launched a rocket that caromed out of bounds at the St. Louis six.

Six plays later, Brooks made his game-sealing play.

**ABOVE: Bucs running back Michael Pittman finds a hole between St. Louis defenders Tommy Polley, front left, and Damione Lewis, back right, during the first quarter.** Gary W. Green/Orlando Sentinel

|            | **1**st | **2**nd | **3**rd | **4**th | **Final** |
|------------|------|------|------|------|-------|
| **St Louis**   | 7 | 0 | 0 | 7 | **26** |
| **Tampa Bay**  | 3 | 10 | 0 | 13 | **20** |

## SCORING SUMMARY

| Qtr | Team | Play | | Time |
|-----|------|------|--|------|
| **1st** | Buccaneers | FG | Gramatica 39-yd. field goal ...................................................... | 9:37 |
| **1st** | Rams | TD | Faulk 5-yd. run (Wilkins kick) ................................................ | 4:34 |
| **2nd** | Buccaneers | FG | Gramatica 47-yd. field goal ................................................ | 15:00 |
| **2nd** | Buccaneers | TD | Dudley 9-yd. pass from B. Johnson (Gramatica kick) ............ | 1:02 |
| **4th** | Buccaneers | TD | Alstott 2-yd. run (2-pt. conv. fails) ...................................... | 10:49 |
| **4th** | Rams | TD | Gordon 21-yd. run (Wilkins kick) ......................................... | 4:29 |
| **4th** | Buccaneers | TD | Brooks 39-yd. interception return (Gramatica kick) .............. | 1:09 |

## OFFENSE

### RAMS

| PASSING | COMP | ATT | YDS | TD | INT |
|---------|------|-----|-----|----|-----|
| Warner | 30 | 45 | 301 | 0 | 4 |

| RECEIVING | REC | YDS | TD |
|-----------|-----|-----|----|
| Holt | 12 | 139 | 0 |
| Bruce | 4 | 43 | 0 |
| Proehl | 4 | 31 | 0 |
| Faulk | 2 | 27 | 0 |
| Conwell | 2 | 20 | 0 |
| Gordon | 2 | 15 | 0 |
| Murphy | 2 | 11 | 0 |
| Wilkins | 1 | 10 | 0 |
| Candidate | 1 | 5 | 0 |

| RUSHING | ATT | YDS | TD |
|---------|-----|-----|----|
| Gordon | 4 | 44 | 1 |
| Warner | 3 | 19 | 0 |
| Candidate | 6 | 15 | 0 |
| Faulk | 6 | 9 | 1 |
| Wilkins | 1 | 2 | 0 |

### BUCCANEERS

| PASSING | COMP | ATT | YDS | TD | INT |
|---------|------|-----|-----|----|-----|
| B. Johnson | 23 | 32 | 199 | 1 | 0 |

| RECEIVING | REC | YDS | TD |
|-----------|-----|-----|----|
| K. Johnson | 4 | 59 | 0 |
| Dilger | 5 | 38 | 0 |
| McCardell | 3 | 28 | 0 |
| Pittman | 6 | 28 | 0 |
| Yoder | 1 | 16 | 0 |
| Alstott | 1 | 10 | 0 |
| Williams | 1 | 5 | 0 |

| RUSHING | ATT | YDS | TD |
|---------|-----|-----|----|
| Pittman | 11 | 53 | 0 |
| Alstott | 5 | 10 | 1 |

**ABOVE:** Bucs running back Mike Alstott bowls over Rams defenders Tommy Polley, right, and Grant Wistrom for a touchdown in the fourth quarter. The touchdown put the Bucs up 19-7.
Gary W. Green/Orlando Sentinel

## TAMPA BAY 35
### GAME FOUR
## CINCINNATI 7

# BUCS BLOW OUT BENGALS

**BY CHRIS HARRY, ORLANDO SENTINEL**

It had been more than two years since the Tampa Bay Buccaneers went on the road and trashed an inferior opponent.

OK, so those were the Cincinnati Bengals on the backside of a 35-7 beating Sunday before a crowd of 57,234 at Paul Brown Stadium. Big deal, right?

But one of the sharpest criticisms of the Bucs during the past two seasons under Tony Dungy was the confounding and infuriating way they managed to play down to their competition. And while it would be easy to assume that no one could play down to level of the Bengals—the NFL's runaway winner as worst franchise—the Bucs must be commended for going on the road and dominating a bad team the way championship contenders are supposed to.

Brad Johnson shook off a first-quarter interception that was returned for a touchdown to pass for 277 yards and three scores, and the Bucs' defense yielded no points and less than 200 yards for the second consecutive road game.

"There was no let-up in us," said defensive tackle Warren Sapp, who had two sacks and a forced fumble for a unit that overwhelmed Bengals quarterback Akili Smith in his first start of the season. "We're surging now. That's what we wanted to do."

On a day when unbeaten New Orleans went to winless Detroit and lost and unbeaten Carolina fell at Green Bay, the Bucs (3-1) pulled into a first-place tie with the Saints and Panthers in the NFC South, with a crucial division game at Atlanta next week.

"The NFL season is a marathon," strong safety John Lynch said. "Now we've got to go on the road—again—and prove we can handle success. That's a big game next week."

The Bengals (0-4), meanwhile, are winless through four games for the third time in four years and the sixth time since 1991, and looked like a disorganized mess. Cincinnati's offense has scored just 16 points in four games.

"You can't win at this level making the kinds of silly mistakes we made," coach Dick LeBeau said.

"We've been losing and losing badly for four years," said Smith, who was 12 of 33 for 117 yards. "It seems like we put together a good game plan every week, but then something happens."

The Bengals have been outscored 119-23 during their 0-4 start. The other five times they started 0-4 since 1991, they won no more than four games.

LeBeau was noncommittal about who would start at quarterback next week.

Johnson, engineer of an offense maligned for its conservative nature the past two seasons, shook off linebacker Brian Simmons's 51-yard interception return to throw touchdown passes of 35 yards to tight end Rickey Dudley, 65 yards to wide receiver Keenan McCardell, and 22 yards to tight end Ken Dilger, proving a downfield passing element does exist for Tampa Bay.

**OPPOSITE: Bucs tight end Rickey Dudley pushes away Bengals defender Jeff Burris on his way to a 35-yard touchdown reception in the second quarter.**
Al Behrman, AP/Wide World Photos

Bucs receiver Keenan McCardell jumps in the arms of center Jeff Christy after scoring on a 65-yard pass reception in the second quarter.
Al Behrman, AP/Wide World Photos

"We took some shots," Coach Jon Gruden said.

Bucs linebacker Shelton Quarles had a 25-yard interception return with 52 seconds left before halftime to give the Bucs a 21-7 lead; it was the third consecutive game the defense has scored on an interception return.

With Quarles's play, the Bucs took total control. At halftime, Tampa Bay had outgained Cincinnati 251-48, limited tailback Corey Dillon to 13 yards on nine carries and held the Bengals on all seven third-down conversion attempts. With Sapp and friends in his face, Smith was just three of 13 for 27 yards in the first half.

"Teams that are 'oh-fer' are going to give everything they got to get that first win, especially at home, but we weren't going to fall victim to that," Bucs linebacker Derrick Brooks said. "Coach Gruden warned us all week, and we sort of took it personally."

RIGHT: Bucs quarterback Brad Johnson throws a pass under pressure from Bengals defender Reinard Wilson in the first half. Johnson completed 19/30 passes and threw three touchdown passes in the game. Tom Uhlman, AP/Wide World Photos

|              | 1st | 2nd | 3rd | 4th | Final |
|--------------|-----|-----|-----|-----|-------|
| Tampa Bay    | 0   | 21  | 7   | 7   | 35    |
| Cincinnati   | 7   | 0   | 0   | 0   | 7     |

## SCORING SUMMARY

| Qtr | Team | Play | | Time |
|-----|------|------|---|------|
| 1st | Bengals | TD | Simmons 51-yd. interception return (Rackers kick) .............. | 2:32 |
| 2nd | Buccaneers | TD | Dudley 35-yd. pass from B. Johnson (Gramatica kick) ....... | 15:00 |
| 2nd | Buccaneers | TD | McCardell 65-yd. pass from B. Johnson (Gramatica kick) .... | 7:45 |
| 2nd | Buccaneers | TD | Quarles 25-yd. interception return (Gramatica kick) ............. | 1:01 |
| 3rd | Buccaneers | TD | Dilger 22-yd. pass from B. Johnson (Gramatica kick) ........ | 10:54 |
| 4th | Buccaneers | TD | Alstott 1-yd. run (Gramatica kick) ....................................... | 3:12 |

## OFFENSE

### BUCCANEERS

| PASSING | COMP | ATT | YDS | TD | INT |
|---------|------|-----|-----|----|----|
| B. Johnson | 19 | 30 | 277 | 3 | 2 |

| RECEIVING | REC | YDS | TD |
|-----------|-----|-----|----|
| McCardell | 4 | 108 | 1 |
| K. Johnson | 5 | 56 | 0 |
| Dudley | 1 | 35 | 1 |
| Dilger | 2 | 33 | 1 |
| Pittman | 5 | 27 | 0 |
| Jurevicius | 1 | 12 | 0 |
| Alstott | 1 | 6 | 0 |

| RUSHING | ATT | YDS | TD |
|---------|-----|-----|----|
| Pittman | 19 | 54 | 0 |
| Alstott | 7 | 29 | 1 |
| Stecker | 1 | 14 | 0 |
| B. Johnson | 1 | 4 | 0 |

### BENGALS

| PASSING | COMP | ATT | YDS | TD | INT |
|---------|------|-----|-----|----|----|
| Smith | 12 | 33 | 117 | 0 | 1 |

| RECEIVING | REC | YDS | TD |
|-----------|-----|-----|----|
| Warrick | 4 | 51 | 0 |
| Bennett | 4 | 27 | 0 |
| Houshmandzadeh | 2 | 20 | 0 |
| Williams | 1 | 15 | 0 |
| Schobel | 1 | 4 | 0 |

| RUSHING | ATT | YDS | TD |
|---------|-----|-----|----|
| Dillon | 21 | 59 | 0 |
| Neal | 2 | 10 | 0 |
| Smith | 4 | 5 | 0 |
| Bennett | 2 | 0 | 0 |

**RIGHT:** Bucs linebacker Shelton Quarles runs past Bengals offensive lineman Matt O'Dwyer after intercepting a pass in the second quarter. Quarles returned the interception for a touchdown.
Tom Uhlman, AP/Wide World Photos

# RONDE
# BARBER

## Barber is Now Bona Fide Star

**CHRIS HARRY, ORLANDO SENTINEL**

Surrounded by reporters asking to relive his career afternoon, Tampa Bay cornerback Ronde Barber was more than happy to talk about some of the eye-opening plays he made last week against the Baltimore Ravens.

But not without speaking about the ones he didn't make. Or almost didn't.

Like that pass in the fourth quarter. As a cornerback in the Buccaneers' disciplined Cover 2 defense, Barber is asked to play a physical sort of man-to-man coverage at the line of scrimmage, ideally jamming the receiver to the inside, where linebackers are waiting.

If his assigned receiver releases up the sideline, he must rely on technique, such as putting a hand on the back and leaving it there (without any pushing, of course), tracking the player until he can recover and get back in position.

That's exactly what happened Sunday while working against Baltimore wide receiver Brandon Stokley in the third quarter. Stokley beat Barber off the line.

But Barber was able to force Stokley to the outside, regain position, turn his head at the last instant and bat away a pass that could have gone for a 35-yard completion.

"A plus and a minus on the same play," Barber said.

But as is most often the case with Barber, the plus was on the back end of the play—the preferred side for a defensive coordinator.

"Ronde Barber is playing some great football," Bucs coordinator Monte Kiffin said. "And he's been doing that for a few years now."

Barber's line in the 25-0 win over the Ravens: five tackles and six pass break-ups.

"I'm in position to make a lot of plays," said Barber, in his sixth season out of Virginia. "I think that might even be more important than actually making the plays."

Two years ago, Barber had the kind of season—97 tackles, two interceptions, 20 passes defended, five and a half sacks—that might have landed a more established cornerback in the Pro Bowl.

Last year, Barber made sure he wouldn't be ignored: a league-best 10 interceptions (one returned for a touchdown), 91 tackles and 29 pass break-ups. Those numbers landed him in Hawaii and helped provide Tampa Bay's big-play defensive back with an identity other than "Tiki's brother."

Any discussions about the best cornerbacks in the NFL—Charles Woodson, Aeneas Williams, Troy Vincent, Chris McAllister and Champ Bailey, to name a few—now must include Barber.

In fact, at least one of his teammates went a step further, suggesting that conversations about where Barber compares to the rest of the NFL's personnel should not be limited to cornerback.

"You show me a player who's playing better football at any position in the league right now. People are asleep on this guy." Bucs strong safety John Lynch said. "We've got so many other guys people talk about, but Ronde Barber deserves recognition."

In a season-opening overtime loss to New Orleans, the Tampa Bay defense started like slugs. They allowed two long scoring drives for field goals in the first half and surrendered a long touchdown pass in each half. But upon reviewing the tape, Lynch and his teammates saw Barber playing at a different level than the rest of the unit.

"No one on our defense really stood out," Lynch said.

"Then you turned the film on and No. 20 was all over the field. I think we sort of drew inspiration from that."

At Baltimore, it was more of the same.

"I'm seeing the ball really well right now," Barber said. "That's something I work on all the time."

In the locker room after the shutout, secondary coach Mike Tomlin seemed unimpressed by what he'd seen from Barber that afternoon.

"That's our expectation level for him, but more important, it's the expectation level he has for himself," Tomlin said. "Ronde's standards are high, and he comes out every week to play to them.

"Sometimes you have to ask yourself, 'Is he hot? Or is that just his game?' Well, I think we're finding that's just his game. I believe that—and I believe he believes it."

A lot of that is because Barber doesn't concentrate or dwell in his successes. It's a perfect mentality for a cornerback, whose memory needs to be short.

Except when it comes to learning. And retaining.

"It's easy to glorify the good ones and forget about the bad ones, but the good players glorify the bad ones and forget the good ones," Barber said.

"Knowing where you have to make improvements—that, to me, is the easiest part of this game.

"You can always get better."

Gary Bogdon/Orlando Sentinel

## TAMPA BAY 20
### GAME FIVE
## ATLANTA 6

# THE DEFENSE GETS OFFENSIVE

**BY CHRIS HARRY, ORLANDO SENTINEL**

The Tampa Bay Buccaneers are on a defensive roll that ranks among the best in team history. That's saying something. Not only are they stopping opposing offenses, they're outscoring them, too. And now they're leaving quarterbacks in their wake.

Defensive tackle Warren Sapp intercepted backup quarterback Doug Johnson at the line of scrimmage, then pitched a lateral to linebacker Derrick Brooks, who raced 15 yards for a fourth-quarter touchdown Sunday that sealed a 20-6 victory over the Atlanta Falcons in front of 68,936 at the Georgia Dome.

It was the fourth consecutive victory for Tampa Bay (4-1), as well as the fourth game in a row in which the Bucs have scored a defensive touchdown. The Bucs have scored one defensive touchdown in each of their road games this season; remarkably, that's three more touchdowns than the Bucs have given up in those games.

"We came, we landed, we conquered," defensive end Simeon Rice said.

Along the way, the Bucs knocked Falcons starting quarterback Michael Vick from the game. With the score tied at three, Rice crashed down on Vick for one of his two sacks, sending him from the game with a slight separation of his right (non-throwing) shoulder.

From there, Tampa Bay closed the door behind a 76-yard touchdown pass from Brad Johnson to Keyshawn Johnson, then iced it by foiling a Falcons fake punt. They finished matters with Brooks's touchdown, his third of the year—which makes him the leading scorer on the team.

Leave it to Sapp, Brooks and company to show up Keyshawn Johnson, who caught six passes for 131 yards—his touchdown was the longest reception of his seven-season career—in one of his finest days as a Buc.

"It's a great run," Tampa Bay coach Jon Gruden said of the winning streak. "We don't want to diminish what they've accomplished, but at the same time, we're going to keep raising the bar."

Defensively, the Bucs were ultra-disciplined in their assignments and never let Vick break containment or find a rhythm before sending him to the sidelines. Vick finished four of 12 for 37 yards and ran once for a yard.

On a day when the Bucs again struggled to run the ball and were back to their inconsistent ways on offense, the defense limited the Falcons to 243 yards of offense and forced four interceptions, including three by former Florida starter Doug Johnson.

The other interception came when punter Chris Mohr appeared to have fooled the Bucs for a fourth-and-nine completion to Brian Kozlowski out of punt formation. But free safety Dexter Jackson arrived at the same time as the pass, knocking it into the air, and Dwight Smith came down with the interception 19 yards downfield.

"We have some deadly bullets on this team, and we're going shooting," Sapp said. "[Gruden] says there should be an investigation 'cause it looks like there are 12 of us out there right now."

**ABOVE:** Bucs receiver Keyshawn Johnson tries to break free from Falcons cornerback Juran Bolden after making a catch in the second quarter. Alan Mothner, AP/Wide World Photos

**ABOVE:** Warren Sapp reacts after he intercepted a pass and pitched it to Derrick Brooks, who ran it in for a touchdown in the fourth quarter.

Alan Mothner, AP/Wide World Photos

**RIGHT:** Bucs quarterback Brad Johnson is brought down by Falcons linebacker Matt Stewart in the second quarter.

Alan Mothner, AP/Wide World Photos

| | 1st | 2nd | 3rd | 4th | Final |
|---|---|---|---|---|---|
| Tampa Bay | 0 | 3 | 7 | 10 | 20 |
| Atlanta | 3 | 0 | 3 | 0 | 6 |

## SCORING SUMMARY

| Qtr | Team | Play | | Time |
|---|---|---|---|---|
| 1st | Falcons | FG | Feely 34-yd. field goal | 7:09 |
| 2nd | Buccaneers | FG | Gramatica 23-yd. field goal | 8:07 |
| 3rd | Falcons | FG | Feely 32-yd. field goal | 6:22 |
| 3rd | Buccaneers | TD | K. Johnson 76-yd. pass from B. Johnson (Gramatica kick) | 4:43 |
| 4th | Buccaneers | FG | Gramatica 22-yd. field goal | 6:34 |
| 4th | Buccaneers | TD | Brooks 15-yd. interception return (Gramatica kick) | 6:24 |

## OFFENSE

### BUCCANEERS

| PASSING | COMP | ATT | YDS | TD | INT |
|---|---|---|---|---|---|
| B. Johnson | 17 | 31 | 261 | 1 | 1 |

| RECEIVING | REC | YDS | TD |
|---|---|---|---|
| K. Johnson | 6 | 131 | 1 |
| McCardell | 6 | 83 | 0 |
| Jurevicius | 1 | 19 | 0 |
| Cook | 1 | 13 | 0 |
| Pittman | 2 | 9 | 0 |
| Alstott | 1 | 6 | 0 |

| RUSHING | ATT | YDS | TD |
|---|---|---|---|
| Pittman | 19 | 62 | 0 |
| Alstott | 4 | 9 | 0 |
| McCardell | 1 | 3 | 0 |
| B. Johnson | 1 | 2 | 0 |
| Stecker | 1 | -2 | 0 |

### FALCONS

| PASSING | COMP | ATT | YDS | TD | INT |
|---|---|---|---|---|---|
| Johnson | 13 | 25 | 150 | 0 | 3 |
| Vick | 4 | 12 | 37 | 0 | 0 |
| Mohr | 0 | 1 | 0 | 0 | 1 |

| RECEIVING | REC | YDS | TD |
|---|---|---|---|
| Finneran | 5 | 61 | 0 |
| Duckett | 3 | 34 | 0 |
| Jefferson | 2 | 32 | 0 |
| Kozlowski | 2 | 17 | 0 |
| Jackson | 1 | 16 | 0 |
| Dunn | 2 | 13 | 0 |
| Crumpler | 1 | 9 | 0 |
| Kelly | 1 | 5 | 0 |

| RUSHING | ATT | YDS | TD |
|---|---|---|---|
| Duckett | 11 | 52 | 0 |
| Dunn | 9 | 14 | 0 |
| Johnson | 1 | 3 | 0 |
| Vick | 1 | 1 | 0 |

**ABOVE: Falcons quarterback Michael Vick is stopped by Bucs defensive lineman Anthony McFarland as Todd McClure of the Falcons looks on in the second quarter.** Alan Mothner, AP/Wide World Photos

# CLEVELAND 3
## GAME SIX
# TAMPA BAY 17

# BUCS BECOME "NASTY BUNCH"

**BY CHRIS HARRY, ORLANDO SENTINEL**

Go ahead, criticize the Tampa Bay Buccaneers. Point out their obvious shortcomings, if you must. But do so with the understanding that no team in the franchise's 27-year history has had a better record at this stage of the season.

As their defensive rampage continued, the Bucs got a lift Sunday from their missing-in-action running game. Fullback Mike Alstott rushed for 126 yards and two touchdowns in a 17-3 victory against the Cleveland Browns before a sold-out crowd of 65,627 at Raymond James Stadium.

Alstott sparked an offense that steamrolled to 186 rushing yards. That was more than enough cushion for a defense that yielded 194 total yards to the league's 10th-ranked offense and kept a third consecutive opponent—and the fourth in five games—out of the end zone in winning for the fifth consecutive week.

"Right now, the defense is the story," Tampa Bay cornerback Ronde Barber said. "You're going to be talking about us for a long time."

The Bucs (5-1) equaled the best six-game start in team history, matching those by the 1979 and '97 versions; both opened their seasons with five consecutive victories.

And Barber's right: the defense has been the story. Tampa Bay has allowed only two touchdowns in the past 22 quarters, dating to the season-opening loss to the New Orleans Saints.

For anybody else, this would constitute a roll, but Tampa Bay has perspective. "Let's be honest here," defensive tackle Warren Sapp said. "It's not like we've been playing 'Air Coryell' now."

The combined record of Bucs opponents during their five-game winning streak is 7-21. But consider how the NFL world will take notice if that string of scoreless quarters swells next week when Tampa Bay visits Philadelphia, where the past two Buccaneers seasons have ended in hideous fashion.

"We'll take a day or two to enjoy this one, but we think we'll be ready for that one," strong safety John Lynch said.

The Bucs led 10-0 at halftime and held the Browns to 97 total yards in the first half. That was four more than the Browns had at the end of the third quarter.

"That's been their MO," Browns coach Butch Davis said of the Bucs. "They get a lead, then just grind you and pound away."

The Browns (2-4) finished with 60 rushing yards and 11 first downs. "We play hard. We play fast. We play physical," Barber said.

But they don't play perfect. Brad Johnson completed less than 50 percent of his throws—15 of 32

---

**OPPOSITE: Bucs defenders Ronde Barber, left, and Nate Webster, right, flip Cleveland tight end Steve Heiden head over heels in the fourth quarter of the Bucs' 17-3 victory over the Browns.** Gary W. Green/Orlando Sentinel

**Bucs quarterback Brad Johnson gets a pass off just as he is hit by Steve Heiden of the Browns.**
John Raoux/ Orlando Sentinel

for 194 yards, no touchdowns and one interception—and the field-goal team missed one kick, had one blocked and flubbed the snap on a third.

"We may not have put it all together on offense, but we got the running game going, and that's a big start," guard Cosey Coleman said. "That's a big boost for us."

The defense, meanwhile, remains a given.

And, to repeat, no Bucs team ever has been better.

**ABOVE:** Jon Gruden argues with an official over an unsportsmanlike-conduct call against the Bucs.

John Raoux/ Orlando Sentinel

| | 1st | 2nd | 3rd | 4th | Final |
|---|---|---|---|---|---|
| Cleveland | 0 | 0 | 0 | 3 | 3 |
| Tampa Bay | 7 | 3 | 0 | 7 | 17 |

## SCORING SUMMARY

| Qtr | Team | Play | | Time |
|---|---|---|---|---|
| 1st | Buccaneers | TD | Alstott 1-yd. run (Gramatica kick) | 9:05 |
| 2nd | Buccaneers | FG | Gramatica 33-yd. field goal | 2:46 |
| 4th | Buccaneers | TD | Alstott 17-yd. run (Gramatica kick) | 15:00 |
| 4th | Browns | FG | Dawson 50-yd. field goal | 11:50 |

## OFFENSE

### BROWNS

| PASSING | COMP | ATT | YDS | TD | INT |
|---|---|---|---|---|---|
| Couch | 20 | 40 | 151 | 0 | 1 |

| RECEIVING | REC | YDS | TD |
|---|---|---|---|
| Northcutt | 4 | 74 | 0 |
| White | 10 | 34 | 0 |
| Morgan | 2 | 16 | 0 |
| Heiden | 1 | 12 | 0 |
| Johnson | 2 | 11 | 0 |
| Davis | 1 | 4 | 0 |

| RUSHING | ATT | YDS | TD |
|---|---|---|---|
| White | 9 | 38 | 0 |
| Green | 8 | 22 | 0 |
| Morgan | 1 | 0 | 0 |

### BUCCANEERS

| PASSING | COMP | ATT | YDS | TD | INT |
|---|---|---|---|---|---|
| B. Johnson | 15 | 32 | 194 | 0 | 1 |

| RECEIVING | REC | YDS | TD |
|---|---|---|---|
| Pittman | 5 | 95 | 0 |
| K. Johnson | 4 | 64 | 0 |
| Alstott | 2 | 13 | 0 |
| Dilger | 2 | 12 | 0 |
| McCardell | 1 | 7 | 0 |
| Dudley | 1 | 3 | 0 |

| RUSHING | ATT | YDS | TD |
|---|---|---|---|
| Alstott | 17 | 126 | 2 |
| Pittman | 16 | 53 | 0 |
| Stecker | 3 | 11 | 0 |
| B. Johnson | 1 | 5 | 0 |
| Tupa | 1 | -9 | 0 |

Bucs defensive tackle Warren Sapp taunts the Browns' offensive line late in the game. John Raoux/ Orlando Sentinel

# MIKE
# ALSTOTT

## Room to Roam

CHRIS HARRY, ORLANDO SENTINEL

**W**hen Jon Gruden first began evaluating the personnel he inherited in taking over the Tampa Bay Buccaneers, he watched tape after tape of Mike Alstott and kept asking himself the same question.

What is this guy?

The debate actually has been raging since 1996, when Alstott was drafted in the second round from Purdue and first climbed into those ghastly Creamsicle uniforms. Gruden became the fourth offensive coordinator to delve into the Alstott dilemma, but he might be the first who accepts Alstott for what he is.

"A very solid football player," he said.

Tampa Bay's quarterbacks aren't the only players who have had to adjust to those four coordinators in four years. In fact, third-teamer Shaun King is the only quarterback to have been with the Bucs through Mike Shula (1999), Les Steckel (2000), Clyde Christensen (2001) and now Gruden.

Alstott has not only seen them all, he's outlasted them.

Along the way, he's been voted to the Pro Bowl five straight times and endeared himself to the pewter faithful through a work ethic and blue-collar style that plays perfectly on NFL Films. That has made him one of the most popular players on the team.

"I work hard," said Alstott, the only starter remaining on the Bucs' offense who dates to the orange days. "I've had a lot of criticism. You can't do this, you can't do that—but I still do it. I love working hard, being out there and trying to make things happen. I'm not a rah-rah guy, just someone who tries to inspire through my play."

Some of the most inspiring and memorable plays of Tampa Bay's newfound era of success — four playoff berths in the past five seasons — have occurred with Alstott carrying the football. The vision of defensive backs bouncing off his 6-foot-1, 248-pound body conjures memories of John Riggins in his heyday.

"I like to think that over those six years I've made a move or two," Alstott said.

Any flashes of shiftiness in the open field probably have more to do with defenders getting shifty (and cold) feet.

"Guys are cringing with fear that they might get run over, if you will, when they approach Mike in the open field; accordingly, they're frozen and lock up," general manager Rich McKay said. "Where Mike makes people miss is later in the game, when he's punished a few people along the way. And don't think they don't see that in the huddle, on the sideline or on the tape the week before."

Those are the plays that fire up a crowd; fire up a team.

"He plays offense the way one of us would," said Bucs linebacker Nate Webster. "And with that big ol' head of his, he could knock some people out if he was playing defense. Maybe he should come over for a couple of plays."

It's been enough of a quandary for the Bucs figuring out Alstott on the offensive side; not that it's brain surgery. The team's all-time leader in touchdowns (40) and No. 3 career rusher (3,982 yards), Alstott has made it quite clear what he does best during his first six seasons. He runs between the tackles and oftentimes over defenders.

Still, almost every off-season there's been a buzz around One Buc Place about Mike Alstott's new role.

"I don't know what else you can do with me," he said.

That's why Gruden intends to play to Alstott's strength. At Oakland, Gruden used a variety of personnel groupings on offense in his versatile and innovative scheme. Just as he did with Napoleon Kaufman, Charlie Garner and Tyrone Wheatley, Gruden will play with the combination of Alstott, free-agent tailback Michael Pittman and rookie Travis Stephens.

The offense will base out of Pittman at tailback and Alstott at fullback, but Alstott also will get looks at tailback and in one-back sets.

If that sounds hauntingly similar to what predecessors tried to do with Alstott and the departed Warrick Dunn, ask yourself who you would rather have devising ways to get Alstott the ball.

Gruden or Christensen?

"Mike, when it's all said and done, will be a guy who has a creative role that will be dependent upon who we're seeing, what kind of defense we're seeing and how we want to attack them," Gruden said.

Truth be told, the Bucs wanted Dunn over Alstott during the off-season but weren't about to match Atlanta's $28 million offer to Dunn. By not doing so, they were able to rework Alstott's contract and sign him to a four-year extension.

"I love it," Alstott said. "I'm living out a dream."

That part of his role is very well defined.

Gary Bogdon/Orlando Sentinel

## TAMPA BAY 10
### GAME SEVEN
## PHILADELPHIA 20

# BUCS' OFFENSE BOTTOMS OUT

### BY CHRIS HARRY, ORLANDO SENTINEL

Put a 50-year-old Sid Gillman on the headsets and Dan Marino in his prime under center. Line up a vintage Walter Payton in the backfield behind Joe Gibbs's "Hogs," then split Jerry Rice and Steve Largent out wide. It still wouldn't matter.

Pewter and red will undermine the best-laid offensive plans. Just ask Jon Gruden.

The Tampa Bay Buccaneers came here Sunday to erase the memories of failures past. Instead, they relived them.

Philadelphia quarterback Donovan McNabb passed for one touchdown and ran for another, and the Eagles' defense proved every bit as dominant as in the past three meetings, holding the Bucs to a measly 207 total yards in a convincing 20-10 victory in front of an unruly sellout crowd of 65,523.

"I'm very disappointed," Gruden said after watching his team's five-game winning streak come to a screeching halt. "I don't even know if that's a good word."

Gruden had watched his team turn in an offensive perfor-

BELOW: Bucs coach John Gruden reacts as he watches the Eagles run out the clock in the fourth quarter. Rusty Kennedy, AP/Wide World Photos

mance that looked like something from Clyde Christensen's playbook. The Bucs (5-2), who fell a game behind first-place New Orleans in the NFC South, failed to reach the end zone on offense for the first time this season and finished with their fewest total yards since gaining 199 in a 21-3 playoff loss here Jan. 31, 2000.

Quarterback Brad Johnson, who had to leave the game in the fourth quarter because of soreness in his ribs, passed for just 124 yards, was sacked five times by Philly's relentless pressure and intercepted once.

Rob Johnson came off the bench and basically ran for his life in passing for 31 yards and getting sacked once.

"Statistically, their defense was No. 1 in the National Football League," Philadelphia coach Andy Reid said. "I firmly believe ours is No. 1."

The Bucs held the Eagles (4-2) and the NFL's fourth-ranked offense to 269 yards, but McNabb and his troops made the plays when they had to and eventually punched through Tampa Bay's run defense. Tailback Duce Staley moved the pile for the better part of the game, then shot off

**ABOVE:** Eagles defensive tackle Darwin Walker sacks Bucs quarterback Brad Johnson during the second quarter. Bucs quarterbacks were sacked six times in the game. Rusty Kennedy, AP/Wide World Photos

ABOVE: Eagles quarterback Donovan McNabb fumbles the ball as he is hit by Bucs defensive end Simeon Rice during the first quarter. Derrick Brooks recovered the fumble and scored a touchdown on the play.
Chris Gardner, AP/Wide World Photos

a 57-yarder with just over two minutes to go, finishing with 152 yards on 24 carries.

"We expect ourselves to play better," Bucs strong safety John Lynch said. "At halftime, we really did feel good, even though we gave them a play."

Simeon Rice's blindside sack of McNabb in the first quarter forced a fumble that linebacker Derrick Brooks scooped up, and he rumbled into the end zone for a 7-3 lead. It was Brooks's fourth touchdown off a turnover this season, and the fifth by an opportunistic Tampa Bay defense.

But it wasn't going to be enough against one of the league's most dangerous offensive weapons.

Though the Bucs held McNabb in check for the better part of the half—the Eagles had just 72 yards through nearly the first 27 minutes—a 29-yard punt return by Brian Mitchell gave Philly a first down at Tampa Bay's 45 with 3:10 left in the first half. On second down, McNabb dropped back behind a maximum-protection

line and heaved a perfect 42-yard touchdown strike to Todd Pinkston, as free safety Dexter Jackson was late coming with help.

The momentum swing was huge and carried over into the second half. So did the Bucs' ineptitude on offense.

The teams traded field goals in the third quarter, but Johnson, smarting from the shot to his ribs, couldn't get enough juice on a sideline pass for Keyshawn Johnson early in the fourth quarter. Al Harris was there for a tiptoe interception. McNabb turned the turnover into a nine-play, 42-yard drive, finishing it off with a one-yard touchdown run that put the Eagles ahead by 10.

"What can I say?" Gruden asked.

"We have to score."

The franchise gave up two first-round picks, two seconds and $8 million for Gruden for that very reason.

And they still can't.

**ABOVE:** Bucs linebacker Derrick Brooks recovered a fumble by Eagles quarterback Donavan McNabb in the first quarter and rushed into the end zone for a touchdown. The play resulted in the only touchdown of the game for the Bucs. Rusty Kennedy, AP/Wide World Photos

|              | 1st | 2nd | 3rd | 4th | Final |
|--------------|-----|-----|-----|-----|-------|
| Tampa Bay    | 7   | 0   | 3   | 0   | 10    |
| Philadelphia | 3   | 7   | 3   | 7   | 20    |

## SCORING SUMMARY

| Qtr | Team | Play | | Time |
|-----|------|------|--|------|
| 1st | Eagles | FG | Akers 30-yd. field goal | 10:32 |
| 1st | Buccaneers | TD | Brooks 11-yd. fumble return (Gramatica kick) | 5:48 |
| 2nd | Eagles | TD | Pinkston 42-yd. pass from McNabb (Akers kick) | 2:37 |
| 3rd | Eagles | FG | Akers 36-yd. field goal | 6:25 |
| 3rd | Buccaneers | FG | Gramatica 48-yd. field goal | 2:43 |
| 4th | Eagles | TD | McNabb 1-yd. run (Akers kick) | 8:24 |

## OFFENSE

### BUCCANEERS

| PASSING | COMP | ATT | YDS | TD | INT |
|---------|------|-----|-----|----|----|
| B. Johnson | 19 | 31 | 124 | 0 | 1 |
| R. Johnson | 4 | 7 | 31 | 0 | 0 |

| RECEIVING | REC | YDS | TD |
|-----------|-----|-----|----|
| K.†Johnson | 3 | 38 | 0 |
| Jurevicius | 3 | 35 | 0 |
| McCardell | 5 | 32 | 0 |
| Dudley | 1 | 18 | 0 |
| Pittman | 4 | 15 | 0 |
| Dilger | 2 | 9 | 0 |
| Alstott | 5 | 8 | 0 |

| RUSHING | ATT | YDS | TD |
|---------|-----|-----|----|
| Pittman | 12 | 49 | 0 |
| Alstott | 5 | 14 | 0 |
| Johnson | 3 | 10 | 0 |
| Stecker | 1 | 8 | 0 |

### EAGLES

| PASSING | COMP | ATT | YDS | TD | INT |
|---------|------|-----|-----|----|----|
| McNabb | 12 | 25 | 127 | 1 | 1 |

| RECEIVING | REC | YDS | TD |
|-----------|-----|-----|----|
| Pinkston | 4 | 61 | 1 |
| Levens | 3 | 37 | 0 |
| Thrash | 2 | 17 | 0 |
| Staley | 2 | 12 | 0 |
| Martin | 1 | 0 | 0 |

| RUSHING | ATT | YDS | TD |
|---------|-----|-----|----|
| Staley | 24 | 152 | 0 |
| Levens | 2 | 9 | 0 |
| McNabb | 6 | 4 | 1 |
| Westbrook | 1 | -1 | 0 |
| Thrash | 1 | -5 | 0 |

**ABOVE:** Eagles quarterback Donovan McNabb rushes into the end zone as Dwight Smith, Simeon Rice, Greg Spires and Warren Sapp give chase during the fourth quarter. Chris Gardner, AP/Wide World Photos

# TAMPA BAY 12
## GAME EIGHT
## CAROLINA 9

# BUCS GET THEIR KICKS (FOUR TIMES)

### BY CHRIS HARRY, ORLANDO SENTINEL

The Tampa Bay Buccaneers hadn't sniffed the end zone all day. Their defense had been dominant and the offense dormant, and there they were, trailing by three points in a field-goals-only affair and lining up to punt with just over three minutes left.

Amid the mess, linebacker and emotional team leader Derrick Brooks ordered every player—healthy or injured, suited up or not—to get off the bench and stand on the sideline.

"Everybody come and see this win," Brooks commanded.

With five seconds left, Martin Gramatica punched a 47-yard field goal through the uprights to give the Bucs a hideous, improbable and wildly energizing 12-9 win over the Carolina Panthers before 63,354 at Ericsson Stadium.

"You can say it was ugly if you want, but for us it was beautiful," reasoned Tampa Bay cornerback Ronde Barber. "It's a big win on the road."

Coupled with Atlanta's upset at New Orleans, the win put the Bucs (6-2)—a week removed from being undressed at Philadelphia—in a tie for first place in the NFC South with the Saints at the midway point of the season.

"I look back to two years ago when there was a team in the Super Bowl—the Baltimore Ravens—who won games just like this," Brooks said.

Replacing an injured Brad Johnson at quarterback, Rob Johnson spent his Bucs starting debut running for his life in going 22 of 33 for 179 yards with one interception. He also was sacked six times by the Panthers, who lead the league in sacks.

"Everybody would like us to be Oakland [on offense], and obviously we're not," Johnson said. "But we're finding ways to win."

Gramatica's 52-yarder with 10:05 left cut the lead to 9-6. But it was his clutch 53-yarder with 1:55 remaining that tied it at nine and gave the visitors reason to believe.

The tying field goal was set up when Aaron Stecker recovered a muffed punt by Pro Bowl return man Steve Smith with 2:53 left.

Carolina (3-5) got the ball back with 1:50 left. But the Panthers' coaches chose not to put the game in the hands of rookie quarterback Randy Fasani, who played as expected in going five of 18 for 46 yards with three interceptions. The Panthers, who have lost five in a row, finished with 130 yards of offense, went one of 12 on third down and saw Fasani sacked three times.

"Our margin of error is not great enough that we can afford to make one mistake," Carolina coach Jon Fox said.

Tampa Bay's margin is only slightly better, and that was enough this time. After the Panthers went three and out, Todd Sauerbrun's 40-yard punt gave the Bucs the ball at their 28 with 1:20 to play.

RIGHT: Warren Sapp and Greg Spires stand over Panthers quarterback Randy Fasani after sacking him in the first quarter. Chuck Burton, AP/Wide World Photos

**ABOVE:** Carolina's Steve Smith (89) looks on as Tampa Bay's Aaron Stecker (27) recovers Smith's fumbled punt return in the fourth quarter. The fumble led to a Tampa Bay field goal.
Chuck Burton, AP/Wide World Photos

Keyshawn Johnson, who had no receptions through the first 58.5 minutes, had back-to-back receptions of 12 and nine yards. A six-yard run from Michael Pittman and six-yard catch by Reggie Barlow got the Bucs into Carolina territory, and on third and nine from the 44, Johnson scrambled for nine yards. But he was hit hard at the first-down marker and had to leave the game.

Enter Shaun King, who coolly hit Karl Williams for seven yards to the Panthers' 28 with 10 seconds left to set up Gramatica's heroics.

"He's our Barry Bonds," Barber said.

"Give him a fastball and he'll give you a three-run homer through the uprights every time."

The Bucs, despite a season-low 226 yards of offense, improved to 6-2 for only the second time in team history. The other time was 1979, when they advanced to the NFC title game.

"We had to find people to make plays for us late in the game, and we did that," Bucs defensive tackle Warren Sapp said. "This was a defining point for this team."

The definition of this team continues to be great defense and no offense. But everyone in pewter and red seems to be fine with that.

"Back to old 'Buc Ball,'" Sapp roared with approval. "Four field goals gets it done."

**ABOVE:** Bucs kicker Martin Gramatica celebrates with holder Tom Tupa after kicking a 47-yard game-winning field goal against the Panthers in the Bucs' 12-9 victory. Rusty Burroughs, AP/Wide World Photos

| | 1st | 2nd | 3rd | 4th | Final |
|---|---|---|---|---|---|
| Tampa Bay | 3 | 0 | 0 | 9 | 12 |
| Carolina | 0 | 3 | 6 | 0 | 9 |

## SCORING SUMMARY

| Qtr | Team | Play | | Time |
|---|---|---|---|---|
| 1st | Buccaneers | FG | Gramatica 32-yd. field goal | 5:00 |
| 2nd | Panthers | FG | Graham 20-yd. field goal | 10:54 |
| 3rd | Panthers | FG | Graham 47-yd. field goal | 8:48 |
| 3rd | Panthers | FG | Graham 39-yd. field goal | 1:38 |
| 4th | Buccaneers | FG | Gramatica 52-yd. field goal | 10:05 |
| 4th | Buccaneers | FG | Gramatica 53-yd. field goal | 1:55 |
| 4th | Buccaneers | FG | Gramatica 47-yd. field goal | 0:05 |

## OFFENSE

### BUCCANEERS

| PASSING | COMP | ATT | YDS | TD | INT |
|---|---|---|---|---|---|
| R. Johnson | 22 | 33 | 179 | 0 | 1 |
| King | 1 | 1 | 7 | 0 | 0 |

| RECEIVING | REC | | YDS | | TD |
|---|---|---|---|---|---|
| Jurevicius | 5 | | 55 | | 0 |
| Dilger | 4 | | 45 | | 0 |
| Stecker | 4 | | 26 | | 0 |
| K. Johnson | 2 | | 21 | | 0 |
| Dudley | 1 | | 15 | | 0 |
| Alstott | 3 | | 11 | | 0 |
| Barlow | 2 | | 10 | | 0 |
| Williams | 1 | | 7 | | 0 |
| Pittman | 1 | | -4 | | 0 |

| RUSHING | ATT | YDS | TD |
|---|---|---|---|
| Pittman | 12 | 36 | 0 |
| R. Johnson | 4 | 17 | 0 |
| Stecker | 5 | 17 | 0 |
| Alstott | 5 | 4 | 0 |
| Williams | 1 | -3 | 0 |

### PANTHERS

| PASSING | COMP | ATT | YDS | TD | INT |
|---|---|---|---|---|---|
| Fasani | 5 | 18 | 46 | 0 | 3 |

| RECEIVING | REC | | YDS | | TD |
|---|---|---|---|---|---|
| S. Smith | 1 | | 39 | | 0 |
| Muhammad | 3 | | 31 | | 0 |
| Hoover | 1 | | 8 | | 0 |
| Walls | 1 | | 7 | | 0 |

| RUSHING | ATT | | YDS | | TD |
|---|---|---|---|---|---|
| L. Smith | 22 | | 82 | | 0 |
| Fasani | 5 | | 15 | | 0 |
| Hoover | 2 | | 7 | | 0 |
| Goings | 2 | | 6 | | 0 |

**ABOVE:** Bucs kicker Martin Gramatica kicks the game-winning 47-yard field goal with five seconds left as Tom Tupa holds and Panthers defender Terry Cousin rushes in.

Chuck Burton, AP/Wide World Photos

# DERRICK
# BROOKS

## Brooks Simply the Best Player in Football

The clamor of Super Bowl Media Day. It is a scratchy album, a clanging cymbal, a grating noise. It is to journalism, someone once said, what rotting road-kill is to 4,000 starving buzzards.

A Don King impersonator is blaring out questions to John Lynch. A horde of fawning New York media is five deep around the podium of Keyshawn Johnson, who is talking about his favorite subject—Keyshawn Johnson.

They crowd around to hear the pearls of wisdom from Simeon Rice, the Tampa Bay Buccaneers' resident philosopher/rapper/poet.

There is standing room only around Warren Sapp, who is holding court as only Warren Sapp can.

But, strangely, wonderfully, there are only a half-dozen of us standing around Derrick Brooks.

He is not a carnival barker like Johnson. He is not a Renaissance man like Rice. He does not have the persona or the pomposity of Sapp.

Derrick Brooks is just the best player in football—that's all.

"I let Sapp do my talking for me," Brooks says of the sparse crowd of reporters around his podium. "I don't believe in talking; I believe in doing."

Does anybody do it better? I don't think so. Brooks is the best tackler in the game, and nobody runs sideline to sideline like he does. There was a game earlier this season when he ran down Marshall Faulk in the open field. New Bucs Coach Jon Gruden couldn't believe it. He grabbed Brooks and began to gush about the play.

"Coach," Brooks said,

"I've been doing this eight years. Relax."

Gruden, it seems, is just like the rest of us. Finally, it seems, we are noticing Brooks. He was chosen the NFL's Defensive Player of the Year, but do you know what he had to do to win it? He had to become the first linebacker in NFL history to return three interceptions for touchdowns. It wasn't enough that he runs and tackles better than anyone; he had to score touchdowns, too.

You wonder how famous Brooks would be if he spent more time talking about himself instead of helping underprivileged kids. Or if he were like Keyshawn, who will tell you he is the best wide receiver in the league even though he isn't. Brooks? He won't tell you he's the best linebacker in the league even though he is.

"That's not for me to say," Brooks says. "That's not what I'm about."

Sapp likes to tell people, "This is my locker room ... this is my team." It is not. There is only one real leader on this team, and his name is Brooks. It his locker room. His team.

Here's all you need to know: Keyshawn doesn't respect Sapp and Sapp doesn't respect Keyshawn. But they both respect Brooks. You ask any Bucs player whom they admire most as a person and a player, and Brooks is the unanimous choice.

In the first game of the season, tempestuous young offensive tackle Kenyatta Walker was deactivated and didn't play. Walker was so angry and embarrassed that he was going to walk out of the locker room before the game and leave the stadium.

Who do you think talked him out of it? Who do you think he listened to? Derrick Brooks.

Who does everybody go to? Who does everybody listen to? Derrick Brooks.

Even Sapp.

"He's the rock in calm waters," Sapp says of his friend and confidant. "Whenever I have a question mark in my life, I go to him and say, 'Brooks, what you got?'"

Super Bowl Media Day blares on. The Don King impersonator is still yammering. Somebody is asking players the age-old question: is your first Super Bowl better than having sex for the first time? Keyshawn is still talking about his favorite subject— Keyshawn. A scratchy album. A grating noise. A clanging cymbal.

And then you go stand next to the best player in football, who is talking about why he spends so much time helping so many underprivileged kids.

"It's my philosophy that if you throw a rope over a fence enough times, somebody's going to grab it," Derrick Brooks says.

Sometimes you don't have to talk real loud to drown out the racket.

## MINNESOTA 24

### GAME NINE

## TAMPA BAY 38

# BUCS DECIDE TO GO ON OFFENSIVE

### BY CHRIS HARRY, ORLANDO SENTINEL

Offensive tackle Kenyatta Walker is in only his second season, but evidently he is well-versed in Tampa Bay Buccaneers history.

Barely 30 minutes after the Bucs had wrapped up a 38-24 foot-wiping Sunday of the Minnesota Vikings, Walker summed up the current state of his team like a seasoned veteran.

"We didn't do nothing special," Walker said. "We knew coming in we were a stronger team. Thing is, a lot of times the Bucs have come in knowing they were the stronger team and [the score] was 6-3. We did what we were supposed to do this time."

Beating the Vikings at home is not surprising, but the way this one played out put a smile on coach Jon Gruden's face.

Quarterback Brad Johnson returned after a week's absence to pass for 313 yards and a career-high five touchdowns, with two to wide receiver Keyshawn Johnson, as the Bucs rolled up a season-best 446 yards before a sold-out Raymond James Stadium crowd of 65,667.

Tampa Bay, 7-2 for only the second time in team history, recovered a fumble on the opening kickoff, converted the turnover into a touchdown and by midway through the second quarter led 24-0.

"This was a big day for us," said Brad Johnson, who missed last week's game at Carolina with a fractured rib and was 24 of 31 for 313 yards with no interceptions or sacks against the Vikings. "We did a great job of making some long drives. The offensive line played tremendously, especially with what I was going through with the rib thing. I don't think I got hit all day."

With protection and time, Johnson fired completions to eight Bucs and threw touchdown passes to four. With No. 2 wide receiver Keenan McCardell (fractured shoulder blade) and No. 3 man Joe Jurevicius (sprained knee and ankle) unable to go, Johnson hooked up for scores with reserve wide receiver Karl Williams from 15 yards, tight end Rickey Dudley from two, Keyshawn Johnson from two and 19 and fullback Mike Alstott from five.

"It's not going to be pretty every week," Keyshawn Johnson said. "But it was pretty this week."

Defensively, the Bucs weren't the heathens who had allowed only six touchdowns in the previous eight games. But they intercepted Daunte Culpepper twice and sacked him three times.

The fumble on the opening kickoff set the tone.

"A great game like that, to start it with a turnover, really sets you back," Vikings coach Mike Tice said.

It took three plays for Brad Johnson to find Williams between two defenders and get the Bucs

---

RIGHT: Keyshawn Johnson was all smiles after catching his first touchdown pass in the second quarter. Bobby Coker/Orlando Sentinel.

**ABOVE: Roman Oben helps Keyshawn Johnson celebrate his second touchdown of the game. Johnson had nine catches, good for 133 yards on the day, as the Bucs beat the Vikings 38-24.**
Bobby Coker/Orlando Sentinel

rolling right away. Tampa Bay scored on its first four offensive possessions for the first time this season.

Minnesota first got on the board when tailback Michael Bennett tore through the Bucs for an 85-yard touchdown run—the longest in Vikings history—and finished with 393 yards of total offense.

"We'll look at the film and see some sloppy stuff," strong safety John Lynch said. "But what offsets that is the win."

The Bucs head into their bye week in sole possession of first place in the NFC South, a half-game up on idle New Orleans. They'll return to the field in two weeks against the Carolina Panthers, in no worse than a first-place tie.

Tampa Bay, Buffalo, Cleveland and Dallas waited the longest—15 weeks, since the start of camp—for their byes.

"It's much-needed," Bucs defensive end Simeon Rice said. "Myself, I need to chill out. I need to be in Barbados or the Bahamas doing something naughty. Now I can do it with a smile."

Gruden talks of playing the 16-game season in four quarters. The Bucs went 3-1 in the first quarter, 3-1 in the second, and are 1-0 in the third. That's a big difference for a team that under former coach Tony Dungy started each of the past four seasons at 3-4 and had to crawl its way back into playoff contention.

"Coach Gruden talked to us after the game about these being the most exciting times of our lives, about having a chance to do something special," Lynch said. "It's in our hands. We've fought uphill in the past, trying to get back in it. Now we're right at the top and everything is in our hands."

For the Bucs, it's a good and altogether different feeling.

**ABOVE: Bucs quarterback Brad Johnson flips a touchdown pass to Keyshawn Johnson. Brad Johnson completed 24 of 31 passes and threw for five touchdowns on the afternoon.** Bobby Coker/Orlando Sentinel.

| | 1st | 2nd | 3rd | 4th | Final |
|---|---|---|---|---|---|
| Minnesota | 0 | 10 | 7 | 7 | 24 |
| Tampa Bay | 14 | 10 | 7 | 7 | 38 |

## SCORING SUMMARY

| Qtr | Team | Play | | Time |
|---|---|---|---|---|
| 1st | Buccaneers | TD | Williams 15-yd. pass from B. Johnson (Gramatica kick) | 13:21 |
| 1st | Buccaneers | TD | Dudley 2-yd. pass from B. Johnson (Gramatica kick) | 1:09 |
| 2nd | Buccaneers | FG | Gramatica 36-yd. field goal | 12:19 |
| 2nd | Buccaneers | TD | K. Johnson 2-yd. pass from B. Johnson (Gramatica kick) | 7:20 |
| 2nd | Vikings | TD | Bennett 85-yd. run (Anderson kick) | 7:02 |
| 2nd | Vikings | FG | Anderson 26-yd. field goal | 0:00 |
| 3rd | Buccaneers | TD | K. Johnson 19-yd. pass from B. Johnson (Gramatica kick) | 5:17 |
| 3rd | Vikings | TD | Williams 1-yd. run (Anderson kick) | 2:10 |
| 4th | Buccaneers | TD | Alstott 5-yd. pass from B. Johnson (Gramatica kick) | 13:39 |
| 4th | Vikings | TD | Williams 1-yd. run (Anderson kick) | 4:44 |

## OFFENSE

### VIKINGS

| PASSING | COMP | ATT | YDS | TD | INT |
|---|---|---|---|---|---|
| Culpepper | 19 | 30 | 231 | 0 | 2 |

| RECEIVING | REC | YDS | TD |
|---|---|---|---|
| Kleinsasser | 3 | 64 | 0 |
| Moss | 4 | 41 | 0 |
| Walsh | 2 | 40 | 0 |
| Williams | 6 | 30 | 0 |
| James | 1 | 29 | 0 |
| Bennett | 3 | 27 | 0 |

| RUSHING | ATT | YDS | TD |
|---|---|---|---|
| Bennett | 10 | 114 | 1 |
| Williams | 7 | 43 | 2 |
| Culpepper | 4 | 8 | 0 |
| Moss | 2 | 8 | 0 |

### BUCCANEERS

| PASSING | COMP | ATT | YDS | TD | INT |
|---|---|---|---|---|---|
| B. Johnson | 24 | 31 | 313 | 5 | 0 |

| RECEIVING | REC | YDS | TD |
|---|---|---|---|
| K. Johnson | 9 | 133 | 2 |
| Dilger | 3 | 61 | 0 |
| Williams | 4 | 49 | 1 |
| Pittman | 1 | 18 | 0 |
| Alstott | 3 | 16 | 1 |
| Barlow | 1 | 13 | 0 |
| Stecker | 1 | 12 | 0 |
| Dudley | 2 | 11 | 1 |

| RUSHING | ATT | YDS | TD |
|---|---|---|---|
| Stecker | 1 | 59 | 0 |
| Alstott | 26 | 55 | 0 |
| Pittman | 3 | 19 | 0 |

**ABOVE: Simeon Rice exhorts the crowd.** Bobby Coker/Orlando Sentinel.

# CAROLINA 10

## GAME TEN

# TAMPA BAY 23

# ALONE AT THE TOP

## BY CHRIS HARRY, ORLANDO SENTINEL

The Tampa Bay Buccaneers won four times Sunday—including once themselves—and today sit alone atop the NFC South Division, tied for the best record in the NFL.

Quarterback Brad Johnson passed for 253 yards and two touchdowns, Martin Gramatica kicked three field goals, and the Bucs' defense ravaged on in a 23-10 beating of the Carolina Panthers before 65,527 at Raymond James Stadium.

The workmanlike effort came after Tampa Bay (8-2) learned that South co-leader New Orleans and Green Bay—now tied for the best record in the league—had fallen earlier in the day, leaving both titles there for the taking, at least for a week.

And as if achieving the best 10-game start in the franchise's 27-year history wasn't enough, the Bucs got the added bonus of an overtime loss by San Francisco, which began the day with the same record as Tampa Bay.

"I'm proud of our team," coach Jon Gruden said after a third consecutive victory. "Granted, some of them aren't the most beautiful things, but there are a lot of ways to win in the NFL."

The one way that will never change is the method of scoring more points than your opponent. Tampa Bay managed to do so Sunday a lot easier than it did three weeks ago in needing four field goals, including the game winner with five seconds left, to beat the Panthers in Charlotte.

Despite falling behind 7-0 on Rodney Peete's 20-yard touchdown pass to Steve Smith in the first quarter, the Bucs shook off the early jolt by moving the ball and capitalizing on turnovers.

Johnson hit Keyshawn Johnson on a fourth-and-goal from the one to tie it at seven in the second quarter. The teams exchanged field goals before halftime and went to the locker room tied at 10.

In the third quarter, the Bucs brought the heat, forcing either three-and-outs or turnovers on Carolina's first five second-half possessions. An interception by cornerback Dwight Smith was converted into a 22-yard touchdown pass to Keenan McCardell for a 17-10 margin.

After another Panthers punt, the Bucs put together a 12-play, 54-yard drive capped by a 32-yard field goal with 8:03 left.

"At that point, it was over," Bucs defensive tackle Warren Sapp said. "Now they got to get away from their running game and Rodney Peete has to beat us from the pocket."

No chance. Against a defense that allowed just 63 yards rushing, Peete went 22 for 38 for 205 yards with three interceptions, four sacks and a fumble. "We never got in any kind of rhythm," Peete said.

RIGHT: Keyshawn Johnson hauls in a pass from Brad Johnson for the first Bucs touchdown as Will Witherspoon and Hannibal Navies of Carolina try to stop him. John Raoux/Orlando Sentinel.

**"** I'm proud of our team. Granted, some of them aren't the most beautiful things, but there are a lot of ways to win in the NFL. **"**

— Bucs coach Jon Gruden after a third consecutive victory

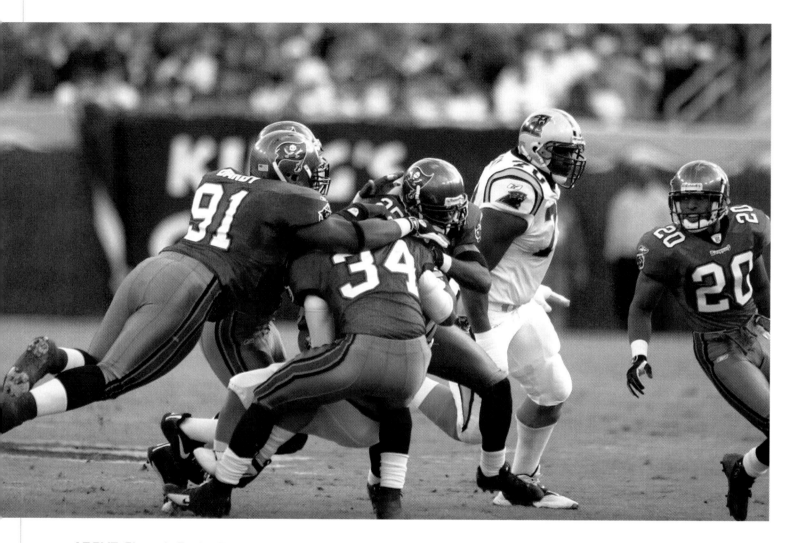

ABOVE: Chartric Darby, Dexter Jackson and the Bucs show the Panthers why their defense is ranked # 1 in the NFL. John Raoux/Orlando Sentinel

The Bucs, with the top-ranked defense in the NFL, weren't going to let them.

There's plenty of work to do—the Bucs still can't run, gaining 67 yards on 29 carries—but the flaws are a lot easier to deal when sitting at the top.

"I'm slow and no good. Brad's over the hill and doesn't have a strong arm. Warren Sapp talks too much. Keenan McCardell is too old. And we don't have a running game," Keyshawn Johnson said. "I can continue to live with it all at 8-2 . . . and just move on to 9-2."

Of the league's other 31 teams, only Green Bay can match that 8-2 record. And the Packers head to Tampa next week.

RIGHT: Warren Sapp celebrates as the defense makes a stop against the Panthers. John Raoux/ Orlando Sentinel.

| | 1st | 2nd | 3rd | 4th | Final |
|---|---|---|---|---|---|
| Carolina | 7 | 3 | 0 | 0 | 10 |
| Tampa Bay | 0 | 10 | 7 | 6 | 23 |

## SCORING SUMMARY

| Qtr | Team | Play | | Time |
|---|---|---|---|---|
| 1st | Panthers | TD | S. Smith 20-yd. pass from Peete (Grahm kick) .................... | 6:15 |
| 2nd | Buccaneers | TD | K. Johnson 1-yd. pass from B. Johnson (Gramatica kick) .... | 9:33 |
| 2nd | Panthers | FG | Graham 42-yd. field goal ...................................................... | 6:30 |
| 2nd | Buccaneers | FG | Gramatica 20-yd. field goal .................................................. | 3:05 |
| 3rd | Buccaneers | TD | McCardell 22-yd. pass from B. Johnson (Gramatica kick) .... | 1:37 |
| 4th | Buccaneers | FG | Gramatica 32-yd. field goal .................................................. | 8:03 |
| 4th | Buccaneers | FG | Gramatica 41-yd. field goal .................................................. | 4:02 |

## OFFENSE

### PANTHERS

| PASSING | COMP | ATT | YDS | TD | INT |
|---|---|---|---|---|---|
| Peete | 22 | 38 | 205 | 1 | 3 |

| RECEIVING | REC | YDS | TD |
|---|---|---|---|
| Muhammad | 3 | 59 | 0 |
| Brown | 6 | 44 | 0 |
| Goings | 4 | 35 | 0 |
| S. Smith | 4 | 30 | 1 |
| Walls | 2 | 21 | 0 |
| Hankton | 1 | 6 | 0 |
| Wiggins | 1 | 6 | 0 |
| L. Smith | 1 | 4 | 0 |

| RUSHING | ATT | YDS | TD |
|---|---|---|---|
| L. Smith | 15 | 46 | 0 |
| Brown | 4 | 17 | 0 |

### BUCCANEERS

| PASSING | COMP | ATT | YDS | TD | INT |
|---|---|---|---|---|---|
| B. Johnson | 22 | 40 | 253 | 2 | 0 |

| RECEIVING | REC | YDS | TD |
|---|---|---|---|
| K. Johnson | 7 | 74 | 1 |
| McCardell | 4 | 56 | 1 |
| Jurevicius | 2 | 48 | 0 |
| Dudley | 1 | 21 | 0 |
| Pittman | 4 | 21 | 0 |
| Stecker | 2 | 20 | 0 |
| Alstott | 2 | 13 | 0 |

| RUSHING | ATT | YDS | TD |
|---|---|---|---|
| Pittman | 21 | 57 | 0 |
| Alstott | 2 | 8 | 0 |
| B. Johnson | 4 | 6 | 0 |

**ABOVE: Michael Pittman finds a hole in the Carolina defense.**

John Raoux/Orlando Sentinel

# MARTIN GRAMATICA

## Gramatica Gets a Kick Out of His Job

BRIAN SCHMITZ, ORLANDO SENTINEL

**Y**ou've surely seen Gramatica The Dramatica. He is the Tampa Bay kicker who looks like he has been handed the winning lottery ticket after making a field goal. A human exclamation point.

Gramatica jumps for joy, runs around crazily and leaps into the arms of teammates. And that's just after hitting one from 20 yards.

If he nails a 45-yarder or a game winner, he needs to be hosed down and checked for hyperventilation. It's often refreshing and comical in the No Fun League. "I think everything shows just how much I enjoy playing," he said.

No kick is too inconsequential to bring out the World Cup wild man in him. It's a wonder he has kept his shirt on. He grew up playing the other football. Goals are so infrequent that soccer players are naturally overcome with emotion.

Gramatica didn't know how truly difficult it was to score, however, until he played for the Bucs. A man must rejoice on those rare occasions, if not take home photographic evidence.

Then it was determined by the surgeon general that too much post-kick partying can be detrimental to your health.

Another kicker tore up his knee last season while celebrating at the field-goal altar. It wasn't just any kicker.

It was Gramatica's brother, Bill.

Now the entire family practice is in question.

But after booting a 42-yard field goal early in a December game against the Giants, Bill jumped high into the air and came down funny on his right (non-kicking) leg. What wasn't funny was a torn anterior cruciate ligament.

Martin regards Bill's injury as a freak accident. Martin ripped his ACL at Kansas State after getting his cleat caught in the turf.

"You can get hurt if you jump or you don't. You're on an island out there," Gramatica said.

He says nobody from the Bucs has advised him to keep his feet on the ground and limit his vertical leap. Countered coach Jon Gruden: "I think that's been addressed after what happened to his brother. I've seen some crazy things happen [in the NFL], b that was in the top 10."

Gruden just wants him to kick responsibly. He doesn't want to curb Gramatica's genuine enthusiasm, because he's an excitable sort himself. "I'm guilty of doing that," Gruden said. "I hope nobody takes offense."

Martin Gramatica has been the most potent weapon for far too long in The Land Where Drives Stall. Fifty-two of his 78 field goals have come inside the 23-yard line, 25 inside the 12. Good thing he's usually "Automatica Gramatica." He is 52 of 57 inside the 39.

"I love kicking extra points," Gramatica laughed.

# GREEN BAY 7

## GAME ELEVEN

# TAMPA BAY 21

# BUCS "WHUP" PACKERS

## BY CHRIS HARRY, ORLANDO SENTINEL

Their defense has been tops in the NFL for the better part of the season, but Sunday the rest of the Tampa Bay Buccaneers joined the fun.

Capitalizing on four interceptions of Brett Favre, the Bucs rolled over the Green Bay Packers on their way to a 21-7 victory before a national television audience and sold-out crowd of 65,672 that witnessed the home team taking sole possession of the best record in the league.

"All eyes are on us," defensive end Simeon Rice said. "We're standing in front of the world and showing everybody what we're all about."

First and foremost, these Bucs (9-2)—in furthering the best start in franchise history—are about defense, but give credit to quarterback Brad Johnson and an offensive unit that seized opportunities and made the Packers (8-3) pay for their mistakes.

What was a frustrating day for Green Bay got even worse in the postgame scene when Packers coach Mike Sherman sought out Bucs defensive lineman Warren Sapp and accused him of throwing a cheap shot and taunting an injured player.

The two had to be separated by players, coaches and team personnel, with Sherman later saying, "Maybe I overreacted."

The coach made it clear, though, that he had a problem with Sapp's hit on offensive lineman Chad Clifton—who was down on the field with numbness in his legs—after leveling him with a block on an interception return.

"I'll bet Coach Sherman had a problem with the [expletive] whupping he got tonight, too," Sapp said.

For the second week in a row, Tampa Bay fell behind by a touchdown at home before rallying for a decisive victory.

"This was a signature game for us," cornerback Ronde Barber said.

"We had a big-time audience tonight and a lot to prove against a good quarterback and we proved it."

Favre, the former NFC Central nemesis who has broken many a Buc's heart during his 12-year career, had the most miserable outing of his five appearances—all losses—at Raymond James Stadium. After completing four of his first six throws for 43 yards and a score to open the game, Favre went 16 of 32 for 153 and the four picks the rest of the way.

"I tip my hat to Tampa. They are a great team. They really, really are," Favre said. "Fortunately, we won't be coming back here for quite some time."

Two interceptions by Brian Kelly, one by Barber and another by free safety Dexter Jackson that went back for 58 yards, either set up touchdowns or stopped potential Green Bay scoring drives. And the Bucs took advantage.

Tampa Bay's offense, meanwhile, may not have lit up the scoreboard, but the Bucs went the distance when it mattered.

**ABOVE:** Tampa Bay's Michael Pittman comes up with a huge catch over the middle for a first down in the third quarter. Green Bay's Tyrone Williams covers on the play.
Gary W. Green/ Orlando Sentinel

ABOVE: Tampa Bay's Warren Sapp gives an earful to Green Bay's Brett Favre after Favre was intercepted in the fourth quarter of the Bucs' 21-7 win over the Packers. Gary W. Green/ Orlando Sentinel

Johnson, who left the game in the first quarter with a scratched right eye, returned to finish 15 of 25 for 134 yards with two touchdowns and no interceptions.

His first scoring strike followed Kelly's first interception and 31-yard runback with the Pack leading 7-6 midway through the third period. Four plays later, Johnson fired a four-yard out to wide receiver Joe Jurevicius, who was first ruled out of bounds. The call was challenged by Bucs coach Jon Gruden and overturned by officials, giving Tampa Bay its first lead. Johnson hit Keyshawn Johnson for a two-point conversion to push the Bucs ahead 14-7.

In the fourth period, Favre badly sailed a pass for Donald Driver into the waiting arms of Jackson, who wove his way to the Packers' three. From there, Johnson bootlegged off a play-fake and hit tight end Ken Dilger

on third and goal for a 14-point margin with 7:24 to go.

Favre's last interception came at the Tampa Bay four, with Kelly draped on Driver and leaping to steal the ball away. Favre reached the shadows of the end zone one last time, but the game ended—fittingly—with Rice sacking Favre as time expired.

"I can't talk enough about the defense," Gruden said after winning his fourth straight and taking a one-and-a-half-game lead in the NFC South on Atlanta (7-3-1) and a two-game lead on New Orleans (7-4), whom the Bucs will face Sunday night on the road. "It really doesn't matter what you call it, whether it's an old-fashioned recipe or cover-two or three-man front, whatever. We're playing very well, very fast and very physical."

And winning.

More than anyone in the NFL.

**ABOVE: Bucs QB Brad Johnson throws a pass in the first quarter. Johnson left the game after getting poked in the eye in the first half. He returned after getting his eye checked out by team physicians.**
Gary W. Green/ Orlando Sentinel

| | 1st | 2nd | 3rd | 4th | Final |
|---|---|---|---|---|---|
| **Green Bay** | 7 | 0 | 0 | 0 | **7** |
| **Tampa Bay** | 0 | 3 | 11 | 7 | **21** |

## SCORING SUMMARY

| Qtr | Team | Play | | Time |
|---|---|---|---|---|
| **1st** | Packers | TD | Driver 4-yd. pass from Favre (Longwell kick) ...................... | 5:44 |
| **2nd** | Buccaneers | FG | Gramatica 38-yd. field goal.................................................... | 0:00 |
| **3rd** | Buccaneers | FG | Gramatica 51-yd. field goal.................................................... | 7:33 |
| **3rd** | Buccaneers | TD | Jurevicius 4-yd. pass form B. Johnson (2-pt. conv. succeeds) . | 5:00 |
| **4th** | Buccaneers | TD | Dilger 3-yd. pass from B. Johnson (Gramatica kick) ............ | 7:24 |

## OFFENSE

### PACKERS

| PASSING | COMP | ATT | YDS | TD | INT |
|---|---|---|---|---|---|
| Favre | 20 | 38 | 196 | 1 | 4 |

| RECEIVING | REC | YDS | TD |
|---|---|---|---|
| Glenn | 4 | 61 | 0 |
| Green | 4 | 40 | 0 |
| Driver | 3 | 32 | 1 |
| Franks | 4 | 29 | 0 |
| Henderson | 2 | 19 | 0 |
| Fisher | 2 | 8 | 0 |
| Walker | 1 | 7 | 0 |

| RUSHING | ATT | YDS | TD |
|---|---|---|---|
| Green | 18 | 56 | 0 |
| Favre | 1 | 17 | 0 |
| Driver | 1 | 16 | 0 |
| Fisher | 3 | 7 | 0 |

### BUCCANEERS

| PASSING | COMP | ATT | YDS | TD | INT |
|---|---|---|---|---|---|
| B. Johnson | 15 | 25 | 134 | 2 | 0 |
| R. Johnson | 3 | 5 | 33 | 0 | 1 |

| RECEIVING | REC | YDS | TD |
|---|---|---|---|
| K. Johnson | 2 | 48 | 0 |
| Jurevicius | 5 | 41 | 1 |
| Pittman | 2 | 23 | 0 |
| McCardell | 3 | 18 | 0 |
| Dilger | 3 | 17 | 1 |
| Williams | 1 | 16 | 0 |
| Alstott | 1 | 8 | 0 |
| Stecker | 1 | -4 | 0 |

| RUSHING | ATT | YDS | TD |
|---|---|---|---|
| Pittman | 13 | 50 | 0 |
| Alstott | 9 | 30 | 0 |
| R. Johnson | 2 | 8 | 0 |
| B. Johnson | 1 | 5 | 0 |

**ABOVE:** The Bucs' sideline erupts after the referee overturned a touchdown catch by Joe Jurevicius, which was originally ruled as out of bounds. Coach Jon Gruden threw the red flag for the referees to review the play on instant replay, which resulted in them overturning the call.

Gary W. Green/ Orlando Sentinel

**TAMPA BAY 20**

**GAME TWELVE**

**NEW ORLEANS 23**

# IT'S A RACE AGAIN IN NFC SOUTH

## BY CHRIS HARRY, ORLANDO SENTINEL

Fasten your seat belts, NFC NASCAR Division fans. The race for the NFC South title is shaping up like a jumbled sprint for the checkered flag, with the Tampa Bay Buccaneers trading paint and checking their rearview mirror.

New Orleans quarterback Aaron Brooks shook off three early sacks to throw two touchdown passes and convert a slew of third downs as the Saints whacked the Bucs 23-20 before a sold-out Superdome crowd of 68,226 and national TV audience.

The outcome wasn't decided until backup quarterback Jake Delhomme, summoned after Brooks left with a strained bicep, hit Joe Horn for a 10-yard completion on third and eight after the two-minute warning, allowing the home team to run out the clock.

"It's a tough league. It was uncharacteristic of us—with the turnovers and mistakes in key situations—in a big game," Bucs coach Jon Gruden said. "I tip my hat to the Saints. They made a lot of big third-down conversions."

The loss was the first in five games for the Bucs (9-3) and left them just a half-game ahead of the surging Atlanta Falcons (8-3-1) in the NFC South and one up on the Saints (8-4), who swept the series and will hold any tiebreakers between the two.

Next week will go a long way toward determining the division crown, as Tampa Bay hosts the Falcons, unbeaten in their past seven games (6-0-1). Atlanta quarterback Michael Vick may be the favorite to win the league's Most Valuable Player award.

With the Bucs trailing 23-12, Brad Johnson moved the offense 84 yards in 17 plays, converting two fourth-down plays along the way, including a two-yard touchdown pass to Keenan McCardell (11 catches, 107 yards) with 2:49 left. Johnson then hit Keyshawn Johnson for the two-point conversion to cut the lead to three. But Delhomme and Horn halted the drama on the next possession.

Brooks was treated rudely at the outset by Bucs end Simeon Rice (three sacks in the first quarter). But Brooks bounced back to throw for 155 yards, including touchdown passes of three yards to Jake Reed and 14 to Horn. Both came on third down.

The Saints, who converted 10 of 20 third-down opportunities in winning 26-20 in overtime at Tampa in the Sept. 8 season opener, went nine of 17 this time, including the game clincher. The Bucs were awful on the "money down," going just two of 14. Brad Johnson and his troops had other issues, too, as the Bucs rushed for a season-low 34 yards on 18 carries against the NFL's only defense to allow at least 20 points in each of its games this season.

**RIGHT: Bucs defensive end Warren Sapp extends his hand to New Orleans Saints quarterback Aaron Brooks at the end of a play in the first half. Sapp pressured Brooks, who threw an incomplete pass.**
Andrew J. Cohoon, AP/Wide World Photos

ABOVE: Saints quarterback Aaron Brooks is sacked by Bucs defensive end Simeon Rice as Warren Sapp gives chase in the first quarter. Rice sacked Brooks again on the next play, setting an NFL record by getting at least two sacks for the fifth straight game. Bill Haber, AP/Wide World Photos

"Right now, we're a little one-dimensional, and it's concerning to me," Gruden said. "But at the same time, there were plenty of opportunities for the Buccaneers to win this game."

Tampa Bay also committed three turnovers.

"It's ridiculous. You can't let that happen," Brad Johnson said. "This game is all about turnovers, moving the chains and making plays. We had a flurry of mistakes. That was the game right there."

The Bucs took a 2-0 lead when Rice got his third sack of the first quarter, forcing Brooks to fumble out the end zone for a safety.

The Saints managed to shake off the play—and hold off Rice—on their next possession, marching 80 yards in 10 plays, with Deuce McAllister (27 carries, 99 yards)

going around the right end for a six-yard touchdown. A try at a two-point conversion failed.

An illegal block on the ensuing kickoff pinned the Bucs at their 10, but Brad Johnson loosened up the Saints' secondary with three short passes, then sidestepped a blitz and fired a 26-yard completion to Keenan McCardell on third and three.

On the next play, Johnson tossed a short pass to Mike Alstott, who turned upfield, got a nice block from Keyshawn Johnson and scored on a career-long 44-yard touchdown reception. Martin Gramatica's point-after made it 9-6.

New Orleans got touchdown passes on its next two possessions to go from three points down to a 20-9 lead with nine minutes left in the third quarter. The Bucs played from behind the rest of the way.

**ABOVE:** Bucs wide receiver Keenan McCardell (foreground) is brought down by Saints defender Sedrick Hodge during the first half.
Andrew J. Cohoon, AP/Wide World Photos

| | 1st | 2nd | 3rd | 4th | Final |
|---|---|---|---|---|---|
| **Tampa Bay** | 2 | 7 | 3 | 8 | **20** |
| **New Orleans** | 0 | 6 | 14 | 3 | **23** |

## SCORING SUMMARY

| Qtr | Team | Play | | Time |
|---|---|---|---|---|
| 1st | Buccaneers | SFT | Safety ................................................................ | 3:24 |
| 2nd | Saints | TD | McAllister 6-yd. run (2-pt. conv. fails) ............... | 10:09 |
| 2nd | Buccaneers | TD | Alstott 44-yd. pass from B. Johnson (Gramatica kick) .......... | 7:02 |
| 3rd | Saints | TD | Reed 3-yd. pass from Brooks (Carney kick) ....................... | 13:00 |
| 3rd | Saints | TD | Horn 14-yd. pass from Brooks (Carney kick) ........................ | 9:06 |
| 3rd | Buccaneers | FG | Gramatica 51-yd. field goal ...................................... | 5:09 |
| 4th | Saints | FG | Carney 48-yd. field goal ........................................ | 9:52 |
| 4th | Buccaneers | TD | McCardell 2-yd. pass from B. Johnson (2-pt. conv. succeeds) ........................................... | 2:49 |

## OFFENSE

### BUCCANEERS

| PASSING | COMP | ATT | YDS | TD | INT |
|---|---|---|---|---|---|
| B. Johnson | 28 | 44 | 276 | 2 | 1 |

| RECEIVING | REC | | YDS | | TD |
|---|---|---|---|---|---|
| McCardell | 11 | | 107 | | 1 |
| K. Johnson | 5 | | 53 | | 0 |
| Alstott | 2 | | 47 | | 1 |
| Pittman | 6 | | 27 | | 0 |
| Jurevicius | 2 | | 18 | | 0 |
| Cook | 1 | | 13 | | 0 |
| Dilger | 1 | | 11 | | 0 |

| RUSHING | ATT | | YDS | | TD |
|---|---|---|---|---|---|
| Alstott | 8 | | 17 | | 0 |
| Pittman | 8 | | 17 | | 0 |

### SAINTS

| PASSING | COMP | ATT | YDS | TD | INT |
|---|---|---|---|---|---|
| Brooks | 9 | 25 | 155 | 2 | 0 |
| Delhomme | 1 | 1 | 10 | 0 | 0 |

| RECEIVING | REC | | YDS | | TD |
|---|---|---|---|---|---|
| Horn | 5 | | 106 | | 1 |
| Reed | 3 | | 43 | | 1 |
| Stallworth | 1 | | 9 | | 0 |
| McAllister | 1 | | 7 | | 0 |

| RUSHING | ATT | | YDS | | TD |
|---|---|---|---|---|---|
| McAllister | 27 | | 99 | | 1 |
| Brooks | 2 | | 5 | | 0 |
| Delhomme | 2 | | -2 | | 0 |

ABOVE: Bucs defensive end Simeon Rice sacks Saints quarterback Aaron Brooks for the second time in the first quarter. Andrew J. Cohoon, AP/Wide World Photos

# KEENAN McCARDELL

## Time to Believe the Hype?

CHRIS HARRY, ORLANDO SENTINEL

**T**he addition of Keenan McCardell gives the Tampa Bay Buccaneers a proven and productive wide receiver opposite Pro Bowl player Keyshawn Johnson—yet another accessory for coach Jon Gruden's sleek, remodeled offense.

But McCardell, a 10-year veteran and former Jacksonville star, brings another important element that should benefit the Bucs. Perspective.

In six seasons with the Jaguars, McCardell was smothered in Super Bowl expectations. After a surprising run from a second-year NFL team to the AFC Championship Game in 1996, the Jags spent four seasons battling the specter of Super Bowl hype as well as opponents.

Sound familiar?

So what advice can McCardell provide a Bucs team that has been dealing with similar pressures the past two seasons.

"Don't listen to it," he said Thursday.

McCardell, 32, signed a four-year, $10 million deal, including a $2 million signing bonus, with Tampa Bay. A salary-cap casualty of the Jags, he took the field with his new teammates for the Bucs' final off-season minicamp.

After the practice, he was asked to talk about big-picture expectations—the kind under which the Jags had crumbled.

"If we just play—and let you guys write whatever you want to write—we just have to go out and execute and not make mistakes by killing ourselves with penalties and turnovers. Do that, and the talent will show," McCardell said. "It's about preparation and hard work. They say the window [of opportunity] closes very fast, but I think you can keep it open if you go out and prepare and stay together as a team."

Preparation, hard work and camaraderie are things Gruden has stressed since jumping to Tampa Bay from Oakland. By all accounts, the Bucs' most prominent off-season additions—running back Michael Pittman, guard Kerry Jenkins, wide receiver Joe Jurevicius, tight end Ken Dilger and McCardell—have fallen in line with that mantra.

"Juice and fire," was how defensive tackle Warren Sapp described the jolt that McCardell gives the offense. "He has a fire that we haven't seen around here, as far as an offensive guy who will talk a little [smack]."

"I've never played with a Pro Bowl-caliber receiver opposite me, one who will draw attention and command respect of a defense," said Johnson, who hauled in 106 passes for the Bucs last season. "This guy comes in here with that."

What McCardell doesn't come with is blazing speed. He's kicked around the NFL since 1991 without it, though.

"It's great to have it, but it's greater to make plays," McCardell said, adding that Oakland's aging tandem of Tim Brown and Jerry Rice did fine minus the jet-burners in Gruden's system last season. "If you run a route right, it's going to look like you have blazing speed."

Added Gruden: "He expresses himself as a route runner sort of differently than some of the bigger guys we have. He's very instinctive, a great hands receiver, very solid after the catch . . . and tough as hell."

Gruden has had his eye on McCardell since it became apparent that the Jags would cut him loose. Expectations for him are very high.

McCardell, though, knows something about hype.

"I'm in catch-up-and-cram mode, but I owe it to them to work as hard as I can," he said. "They're counting on me."

Scott Martin, AP/Wide World Photos

## ATLANTA 10
### GAME THIRTEEN
## TAMPA BAY 34

# DECEMBER BASH

BY CHRIS HARRY, ORLANDO SENTINEL

Four-time Pro Bowl strong safety John Lynch had just wobbled to the sideline with a neck injury in the first quarter, with his team locked in a scoreless tie against the hottest team in the NFL.

Enter backup John Howell, whose two-year career with Tampa Bay has been spent mostly on special teams. Just like that, Howell was breaking the huddle and staring across the line at Michael Vick—Atlanta's lightning-in-a-bottle quarterback—on a third-and-one from the Buccaneers' 39.

As Vick barked the signals, Howell recognized a shift in the backfield, made a read on the quarterback's footwork and inched toward the line. With the snap, Howell shot into the backfield and suddenly was one-on-one against the bootlegging Vick, a TV highlight waiting to happen.

It was a highlight, all right—for Howell and the Bucs, who seemed a step ahead of, and at times even faster than, Vick. Howell's six-yard sack was a defining moment on a Sunday when the soaring Falcons were blasted from their perch as the league's hottest team in a 34-10 defeat before 65,648 at Raymond James Stadium.

"We put so much into our preparation," Howell said after one of the most impressive and complete victories since the team's rise to success in 1997. "We were ready for this team. We were ready for this game. We were ready for Michael Vick."

Vick's rising star was dimmed by a defense that limited Atlanta and the league's next superstar to a measly 181 yards of offense. That same star was outshone by a supernova performance from Tampa Bay's Brad Johnson, who completed 23 of 31 passes for 276 yards with four touchdowns and no interceptions in leading the franchise to double-digit victories faster than any quarterback in the team's 27-season history.

Wideouts Keenan McCardell and Joe Jurevicius each caught a pair of touchdowns, Martin Gramatica added two field goals, and the run-challenged Bucs put together their third-best rushing performance of the season in gaining 150 of the offense's 421 total yards. The team's best all-around offensive display, coupled with another stellar defensive effort, was more than enough to halt Atlanta's unbeaten streak at eight, a run that dated to a 20-6 loss to the Bucs on Oct. 6.

"The defense has been carrying us most of the season," center Jeff Christy said. "It's about time we brought something to the party."

By bouncing back from last week's loss at New Orleans, the Bucs (10-3) maintained a one-game lead on the Saints in the NFC South, opened a one-and-a-half-game edge on the Falcons (8-4-1) in sweeping the

RIGHT: Bucs receiver Keenan McCardell celebrates his first touchdown pass of the day with Keyshawn Johnson. Both McCardell and Joe Jurevicius had two touchdowns on the day. John Raoux/Orlando Sentinel

**ABOVE: Ray Buchanan of Atlanta loses his helmet as he tries to tackle Bucs running back Mike Alstott.**
John Raoux/Orlando Sentinel

series, and remained on pace for a bye and home game in the playoffs.

Tampa Bay also reminded the NFL of something all its followers had momentarily forgotten amid the Michael Vick euphoria.

"He's been hot for eight weeks," Bucs defensive tackle Warren Sapp said. "Our defense has been hot for eight years."

After Vick rocked Minnesota for 173 rushing yards—a league record for a quarterback—and another 173 passing in an overtime win last week, Vick was all the rage. The Bucs, armed with the league's top-ranked defense, took notice.

"All the talk this week was, 'How do you stop Michael Vick?'" Tampa Bay coach Jon Gruden said. "I didn't hear anybody in America say, 'How's he going to go up against this defense?' We haven't been chopped liver since the beginning of the season. We've been playing pretty good around here."

The Bucs did not allow Vick to get going in the last meeting and repeated themselves this time, allowing him just 11 total yards in the first quarter and just 140 for the game (125 passing, 15 rushing). Howell's sack forced a Falcons punt, which Johnson turned into a 10-play, 80-yard march, capped by a 10-yard scoring toss to Jurevicius early in the second quarter. Less than four

ABOVE: The Bucs' Warren Sapp consoles Atlanta's Michael Vick after the Bucs beat the Falcons.
John Raoux/Orlando Sentinel

minutes later, the lead was 14-0 after an interception by free safety Dexter Jackson set up another Johnson-to-Jurevicius strike.

The Falcons got a short Jay Feely field goal at the 2:02 mark before halftime, but a 42-yard catch and run from Michael Pittman set up a big Bucs score just before halftime. When McCardell spun cornerback Juran Bolden and walked in for a 14-yard reception, the scoreboard showed 21-3 with 34 seconds to go before intermission.

Not even Vick had an answer.

"This is the second war of many, hopefully, in my career," Vick said. "This will be my rivalry."

| | 1st | 2nd | 3rd | 4th | Final |
|---|---|---|---|---|---|
| Atlanta | 0 | 3 | 0 | 7 | 10 |
| Tampa Bay | 0 | 21 | 6 | 7 | 34 |

## SCORING SUMMARY

| Qtr | Team | Play | | Time |
|---|---|---|---|---|
| 2nd | Buccaneers | TD | Jurevicius 10-yd. pass from B. Johnson (Gramatica kick) ... | 11:20 |
| 2nd | Buccaneers | TD | Jurevicius 13-yd. pass from B. Johnson (Gramatica kick) ..... | 7:49 |
| 2nd | Falcons | FG | Feely 30-yd. field goal ................................................ | 2:00 |
| 2nd | Buccaneers | TD | McCardell 14-yd. pass from B. Johnson (Gramatica kick) ..... | 0:39 |
| 3rd | Buccaneers | FG | Gramatica 42-yd. field goal .......................................... | 10:01 |
| 3rd | Buccaneers | FG | Gramatica 21-yd. field goal .......................................... | 5:24 |
| 4th | Falcons | TD | Crumpler 5-yd. pass from Vick (Feely kick) ...................... | 11:46 |
| 4th | Buccaneers | TD | McCardell 27-yd. pass from B. Johnson (Gramatica kick) ..... | 8:39 |

## OFFENSE

### FALCONS

| PASSING | COMP | ATT | YDS | TD | INT |
|---|---|---|---|---|---|
| Vick | 12 | 25 | 125 | 1 | 1 |

| RECEIVING | REC | YDS | TD |
|---|---|---|---|
| Gaylor | 1 | 47 | 0 |
| Crumpler | 2 | 25 | 1 |
| Kelly | 2 | 25 | 0 |
| Duckett | 2 | 11 | 0 |
| Jefferson | 2 | 11 | 0 |
| Christian | 1 | 3 | 0 |
| Finneran | 2 | 3 | 0 |

| RUSHING | ATT | YDS | TD |
|---|---|---|---|
| Duckett | 13 | 47 | 0 |
| Vick | 5 | 15 | 0 |
| Christian | 4 | 6 | 0 |

### BUCCANEERS

| PASSING | COMP | ATT | YDS | TD | INT |
|---|---|---|---|---|---|
| B. Johnson | 23 | 31 | 276 | 4 | 0 |

| RECEIVING | REC | YDS | TD |
|---|---|---|---|
| Jurevicius | 8 | 100 | 2 |
| Pittman | 4 | 50 | 0 |
| McCardell | 4 | 49 | 2 |
| Dudley | 1 | 31 | 0 |
| K. Johnson | 2 | 25 | 0 |
| Dilger | 3 | 18 | 0 |
| Cook | 1 | 3 | 0 |

| RUSHING | ATT | YDS | TD |
|---|---|---|---|
| Alstott | 13 | 95 | 0 |
| Stecker | 4 | 30 | 0 |
| Pittman | 9 | 25 | 0 |
| King | 1 | 2 | 0 |

**ABOVE:** Bucs defenders sandwich Falcons quarterback Michael Vick during the Bucs' 34-10 victory over the Falcons.

John Raoux/Orlando Sentinel

## TAMPA BAY 23
### GAME FOURTEEN
## DETROIT 20

# RUMBLING TOWARD THE PLAYOFFS

### BY CHRIS HARRY, ORLANDO SENTINEL

That 10-3 stuff had a nice ring to it last week. To a man, the Tampa Bay Buccaneers liked the sound of it, but coach Jon Gruden had a message for his players.

"If you guys think 10-3 feels good, what do you say we give 11-3 a try?" he said.

Sunday, the Bucs not only found 11-3, they gained an immeasurable appreciation for it following a 23-20 escape act against the Detroit Lions that pushed Tampa Bay into the playoffs for a fourth consecutive season.

Martin Gramatica nailed a 38-yard field goal with 3:04 to play, then watched from the sideline as Lions counterpart Jason Hanson was about five yards short and a bit wide on a desperation 57-yarder that would have tied it with 1:51 left.

Hanson's miss sent the Lions (3-11) to their sixth consecutive defeat, the crowd of 61,942 scurrying for the exits and the Bucs to an 11th win for only the second time in team history.

And that was only half the good news.

In two pivotal NFC South games, the New Orleans Saints lost at home to Minnesota, and the Atlanta Falcons lost at home to Seattle.

Those upset losses mean the Bucs need only to win one of their final two games—at home against Pittsburgh next Monday night or on the road in the Dec. 29 season finale against Chicago in Champaign, Ill.—to clinch the NFC South title and assure themselves of at least one home playoff game. Win both, and Tampa Bay gets a first-round bye.

"One more, and we get to put the hats on," Bucs wide receiver Keyshawn Johnson said. "Who gives a [expletive] what it looked like."

For sure, this one had the look of one of those unforgivable December defeats, the ones that stifle momentum and cripple a playoff run.

"Every way we could find to let them back in the game, we did it," defensive tackle Warren Sapp said. "But you end up winning one you almost gift-wrapped for Christmas."

The Bucs jumped to a 10-0 lead, and Lions rookie quarterback Joey Harrington was gone because of an irregular heartbeat (he was taken to a hospital and believed to be fine Sunday night). But backup Mike McMahon immediately rallied the Lions into a tie.

Though they were without leading rusher James Stewart (knee), the Lions cranked out 144 yards rushing against the league's top-ranked defense, the third most by a Bucs opponent this season. But it was really two plays—a 46-yard pass from McMahon to Bill Schroeder to set up one touchdown and a 91-yard kick-

---

**ABOVE: Bucs kicker Martin Gramatica celebrates with holder Tom Tupa after kicking the game-winning field goal from 38 yards out in the fourth quarter. The Bucs beat the Lions 23-20.**
Paul Sancya, AP/Wide World Photos

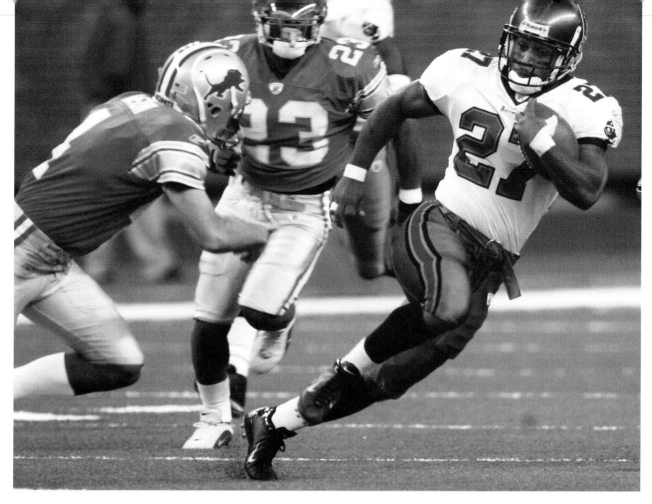

ABOVE: Bucs running back Aaron Stecker returns the opening kickoff 67 yards as he avoids kicker Jason Hanson, left, and outruns Rafael Cooper in the first quarter. Duane Burleson, AP/Wide World Photos

off return from Eddie Drummond to set up the other—that kept the home team in the game.

"Our effort was very high," Detroit coach Marty Mornhinweg said.

And it easily could have been enough.

"This is the National Football League. You can get your block knocked off any Sunday you don't make timely plays," Gruden said. "And when you get beat in the hole of your two-deep zone and give up a 90-yard kickoff return on the road, I wish you luck.

"We were fortunate to win."

With the game tied at 13, Bucs middle linebacker Shelton Quarles stopped a promising Lions drive with an interception. A leaping 30-yard catch by Johnson from quarterback Brad Johnson (24 of 41, 253 yards, no touchdowns or interceptions) set up a four-yard touchdown run by tailback Michael Pittman, his first score of the season.

But the Lions answered with Drummond's return and a two-yard bootleg from McMahon to tie the game at 20 with 9:44 to go.

The teams exchanged punts, and Brad Johnson then marched Tampa Bay to Detroit's 20 before the drive stalled. Gramatica's third field goal of the day proved to be his second game winner this season.

"I'm sure people are going to complain about how we got it done, but you can't always show up in all three phases like we did last week," said linebacker Derrick Brooks, referencing a near-flawless 34-10 home beating of the Falcons. "Sometimes, you got to find a way to win an ugly game."

It's December. How ugly can a victory be?

Especially at 11-3.

RIGHT: Bucs running back Michael Pittman slips away from Lions linebacker Chris Claiborne for a first down in the first quarter. Duane Burleson, AP/Wide World Photos

| | 1st | 2nd | 3rd | 4th | Final |
|---|---|---|---|---|---|
| Tampa Bay | 3 | 10 | 0 | 10 | 23 |
| Detroit | 0 | 10 | 3 | 7 | 20 |

## SCORING SUMMARY

| Qtr | Team | Play | | Time |
|---|---|---|---|---|
| 1st | Buccaneers | FG | Gramatica 20-yd. field goal ................................................. | 10:45 |
| 2nd | Buccaneers | TD | Alstott 1-yd. run (Gramatica kick) ....................................... | 14:21 |
| 2nd | Lions | TD | Schroeder 18-yd. pass from McMahon (Hanson kick) ......... | 11:30 |
| 2nd | Lions | FG | Hanson 37-yd. field goal ..................................................... | 5:39 |
| 2nd | Buccaneers | FG | Gramatica 28-yd. field goal ................................................. | 0:18 |
| 3rd | Lions | FG | Hanson 25-yd. field goal ..................................................... | 12:05 |
| 4th | Buccaneers | TD | Pittman 4-yd. run (Gramatica kick) ..................................... | 10:12 |
| 4th | Lions | TD | McMahon 2-yd. run (Hanson kick) ....................................... | 9:50 |
| 4th | Buccaneers | FG | Gramatica 38-yd. field goal ................................................. | 3:04 |

## OFFENSE

### BUCCANEERS

| PASSING | COMP | ATT | YDS | TD | INT |
|---|---|---|---|---|---|
| B. Johnson | 24 | 41 | 253 | 0 | 0 |

| RECEIVING | REC | | YDS | | TD |
|---|---|---|---|---|---|
| K. Johnson | 6 | | 90 | | 0 |
| Pittman | 5 | | 47 | | 0 |
| Dilger | 3 | | 35 | | 0 |
| Dudley | 3 | | 29 | | 0 |
| McCardell | 2 | | 25 | | 0 |
| Alstott | 3 | | 23 | | 0 |
| Stecker | 2 | | 4 | | 0 |

| RUSHING | ATT | | YDS | | TD |
|---|---|---|---|---|---|
| Alstott | 11 | | 47 | | 1 |
| Pittman | 11 | | 46 | | 1 |
| Stecker | 4 | | 28 | | 0 |
| B. Johnson | 2 | | 2 | | |

### LIONS

| PASSING | COMP | ATT | YDS | TD | INT |
|---|---|---|---|---|---|
| McMahon | 10 | 21 | 158 | 1 | 1 |
| Harrington | 0 | 1 | 0 | 0 | 0 |

| RECEIVING | REC | | YDS | | TD |
|---|---|---|---|---|---|
| Schroeder | 4 | | 96 | | 1 |
| Cason | 2 | | 38 | | 0 |
| Ricks | 1 | | 9 | | 0 |
| Crowell | 1 | | 7 | | 0 |
| Schlesinger | 1 | | 6 | | 0 |
| Anderson | 1 | | 2 | | 0 |

| RUSHING | ATT | | YDS | | TD |
|---|---|---|---|---|---|
| Cason | 10 | | 62 | | 0 |
| Cooper | 8 | | 50 | | 0 |
| Schlesinger | 6 | | 31 | | 0 |
| McMahon | 2 | | 1 | | 1 |

**ABOVE:** Bucs fullback Mike Alstott scores as quarterback
Brad Johnson celebrates in the second quarter.
Paul Sancya, AP/Wide World Photos

# BRAD
# JOHNSON

## The Bull is Back

CHRIS HARRY, ORLANDO SENTINEL

**C**all him determined. Call him competitive. Call him stubborn. Call him willful. Call him any of those things.

That is why his teammates call him "The Bull."

"I've never been around a tougher quarterback," Tampa Bay offensive lineman Todd Washington said. "I'm not sure anybody has."

After missing the final two regular-season games with a back injury, "The Bull" returned in time for the playoffs, where he led the Bucs to victories over the San Francisco, Philadelphia, and Oakland.

The Bucs knew the best chance they had at winning the Super Bowl came with the no-nonsense, 11-year veteran (and all his foibles) under center.

Johnson has his work ethic and a passion to be the best he can be. Admittedly, that passion is taken to extremes at times, but in the NFL, that's not such a bad thing.

"Some quarterbacks have the name and, with it, get the endorsements and go to Pro Bowls and all that, but Brad's just the guy who plays football," Bucs wide receiver Joe Jurevicius said. "He knows that he's good. He's not out there gloating or showing up in the paper every day, but he sure can play the game, and he sure makes us a better team.

"He doesn't show it on the surface, but Brad's got an arrogance about him that he keeps to himself. That's why he's such a good quarterback."

Johnson will be the first to tell you that his arrogance manifests itself in odd ways. This is a guy who from childhood challenged himself to the point of obsession. And still does.

Growing up in the tiny town of Black Mountain, N.C., Johnson played football, basketball and other games against himself. Make 100 bull's-eyes and 300 50-pointers in darts by the end of the day. Throw the football through the tire 20 consecutive times or else run. Take off on a sprint for every missed free throw.

The fixation still rages. Johnson says only a select few—his wife, his best friend and his brother-in-law (Georgia coach Mark Richt, who is married to Johnson's sister)—have any idea of the sort of training regimen he puts himself through in the off-season, away from his teammates. There isn't a Tallahassee resident who hasn't seen Johnson, a former Florida State player, jogging up and down Tennessee Street, but that's only part of it.

The rest he prefers not to talk about.

When it comes time to report for minicamps, Johnson is already in great shape and ready to learn.

Off the field, he is equally meticulous. poring over playbooks and tape until he knows his offense and opposing defenses His attention span is remarkable, too, t the point where Johnson says he has do a study over the years of how quarterback who put their feet up on the table or eat in meetings perform versus those who don't.

"You'd be surprised," he said earnestly.

The surprise is that anyone would think of such a thing. Then again, this is a unique individual who loves everything about what he's doing.

Bucs coach Jon Gruden has spent his career studying and working with quarterbacks. When he arrived, he praised King and signed Rob Johnson to a free-agent contract. But it wasn't long before he learned what the staffs at Minnesota (1992-98) and Washington (1999-2000) already knew, and why the Bucs ponied up $28 million to lure Johnson to Tampa Bay in March 2001.

"He's been like this," said Gruden, using his hand to mark an imaginary and steady line. "Brad has certain, you might say, superstitions, rules or requirements that he has to go through to feel right, certain rituals that work in his own mind. That's OK. He's a rock-solid guy and one of the most consistent human beings I've ever been around."

Some of those rituals: Johnson brings a briefcase to work on game days. Then, he changes jerseys and shoes every quarter, as well as wristbands and towels.

"I'd never want to be Brad's kid," Jurevicius said. "I can't imagine what my room would have to look like. Everything has to be perfect."

Things haven't always been perfect for Johnson on the field. After being sacked a career-high 10 times in a lopsided home loss to Pittsburgh last season, Johnson was hit with a hot dog while leaving the field. A year and a Super Bowl championship later, the guy who threw that hot dog probably appreciates Johnson a little more now.

He'd better.

What matters to the fans should be that Johnson leads the team and runs the offense better than anyone else, and it's not even close.

Craig Jones/Getty Images

## PITTSBURGH 17

### GAME FIFTEEN

## TAMPA BAY 7

# STEELERS BRUISE BUCS

### BY CHRIS HARRY, ORLANDO SENTINEL

The Tampa Bay Buccaneers blew any chance at home-field advantage throughout the playoffs Monday night.

But if their listless and turnover-plagued performance against postseason-bound Pittsburgh was an indication, home field won't help the Bucs next month anyway.

Steelers quarterback Tommy Maddox could do no wrong and Bucs backup Shaun King, summoned for injured starter Brad Johnson, could no right as the Blitzburgh boys came to Raymond James Stadium and throttled Tampa Bay for the second time in as many seasons, dropping the Bucs 17-7 in front of 65,684.

In helping his team clinch the AFC North Division title, Maddox hit 17 of 23 passes for 236 yards, one touchdown and a quarterback rating of 120.9. His counterpart, King, in his first start in nearly two years, connected on just nine of 26 throws for 73 yards with an interception that went for a touchdown. He was benched in the third quarter with a rating of 27.4.

"I think I showed I hadn't played in a while," King said.

Only a meaningless touchdown toss from Rob Johnson to Keyshawn Johnson with 1:14 to go saved coach Jon Gruden from his first shutout as a head coach and his team its first home goose egg since 1996.

"We never got our crowd into the game," said Gruden, whose team trailed by two touchdowns less than

four minutes into the game. "In fact, we probably made them mad after those first five minutes."

The Bucs (11-4) can only hope that Brad Johnson, the NFC's No. 2 passer, can get over his sore lower back in time to make something out of the season.

Maybe even something out of the postseason.

"We're going to have an opportunity to play a home game in the playoffs, we know that," Gruden said.

"When that game is [scheduled] is to be announced."

Considering it turned the ball over three times—twice inside the Pittsburgh 10—Tampa Bay was fortunate to have clinched the NFC South on Sunday when New Orleans was upset by Cincinnati. Though the Bucs are guaranteed of at least a wild-card playoff date at home, they lost control of their fate with regard to the NFC's two first-round byes. One was clinched by the Philadelphia Eagles (12-3) by virtue of Monday's outcome. The inside track to the other was turned over to the Green Bay Packers (12-3).

The Packers must lose next weekend on the road against the New York Jets for the Bucs to have any chance at retaking the No. 2 seed in the NFC. Under that

**RIGHT: Rob Johnson came in for Shaun King at quarterback in the second half but was greeted rudely by Steeler defender Kimo von Oelhoffen.**
John Raoux/Orlando Sentinel

**ABOVE: A frustrated Warren Sapp argues with Chad Brown.**
John Raoux/Orlando Sentinel

scenario, Tampa Bay would have to win next Sunday night against Chicago at Champaign, Ill.

"We'll be pulling very hard for the New York Jets," Keyshawn Johnson said of his former team.

The Steelers made a statement out of the box, going deep on the first play of the game. Maddox, who completed his first seven passes, launched a bomb up the left sideline over cornerback Ronde Barber, who was beaten badly on the play by wideout Plaxico Burress for 41 yards. Burress beat Barber again three plays later on an 18-yard slant play that set up Maddox's 11-yard dart to rookie Antwaan Randle El, who took a quick out and zipped to the pylon for a 7-0 lead less than three minutes into the game.

The lead doubled less than a minute later when King eyeballed Keyshawn Johnson on a sideline route. Cornerback Chad Scott jumped the rout, easily picked the pass and raced 30 yards untouched for a score and 14-0 lead with just three minutes, 50 seconds elapsed.

"Getting off to a 14-0 lead in this type of stadium was very important in keeping the crowd out of it," Pittsburgh coach Bill Cowher said.

After the Bucs went three and out it was more of the same. Maddox fired completions of 20 yards on first down to Hines Ward and 29 to Burress on third-and-five, part of a 70-yard march that ended in a 26-yard field goal from Jeff Reed that made it 17-0 at the 4:24 mark of the opening period.

How different must it have felt on the Tampa Bay sideline? The Bucs had given up 40 points in the first quarter in the previous 14 games combined.

RIGHT: Michael Pittman of the Bucs hangs his head as he sits on the bench during the final moments of the Bucs' 17-7 loss to the Steelers. John Raoux/Orlando Sentinel

|  | 1st | 2nd | 3rd | 4th | Final |
|---|---|---|---|---|---|
| Pittsburgh | 17 | 0 | 0 | 0 | 17 |
| Tampa Bay | 0 | 0 | 0 | 7 | 7 |

## SCORING SUMMARY

| Qtr | Team | Play | | Time |
|---|---|---|---|---|
| 1st | Steelers | TD | Randle El 11-yd. pass from Maddox (Reed kick) | 12:08 |
| 1st | Steelers | TD | Scott 30-yd interception return (Reed kick) | 11:20 |
| 1st | Steelers | FG | Reed 26-yd. field goal | 4:24 |
| 4th | Buccaneers | TD | K. Johnson 18-yd pass from R. Johnson (Gramatica kick) | 1:23 |

## OFFENSE

### STEELERS

| PASSING | COMP | ATT | YDS | TD | INT |
|---|---|---|---|---|---|
| Maddox | 17 | 23 | 236 | 1 | 0 |
| Randle El | 1 | 1 | 8 | 0 | 0 |

| RECEIVING | REC | YDS | TD |
|---|---|---|---|
| Buress | 5 | 127 | 0 |
| Ward | 6 | 78 | 0 |
| Zereoue | 3 | 18 | 0 |
| Randle El | 1 | 11 | 1 |
| Kreider | 1 | 8 | 0 |
| Cushing | 1 | 4 | 0 |
| Bettis | 1 | -2 | 0 |

| RUSHING | ATT | YDS | TD |
|---|---|---|---|
| Bettis | 26 | 66 | 0 |
| Zereoue | 5 | 23 | 0 |
| Randle El | 1 | 4 | 0 |
| Kreider | 1 | 3 | 0 |
| Maddox | 2 | -2 | 0 |

### BUCCANEERS

| PASSING | COMP | ATT | YDS | TD | INT |
|---|---|---|---|---|---|
| R. Johnson | 12 | 18 | 159 | 1 | 0 |
| King | 9 | 26 | 73 | 0 | 1 |

| RECEIVING | REC | YDS | TD |
|---|---|---|---|
| K. Johnson | 8 | 132 | 1 |
| McCardell | 6 | 45 | 0 |
| Jurevicius | 2 | 28 | 0 |
| Dilger | 1 | 11 | 0 |
| Dudley | 2 | 8 | 0 |
| Alstott | 1 | 4 | 0 |
| Pittman | 1 | 4 | 0 |

| RUSHING | ATT | YDS | TD |
|---|---|---|---|
| Alstott | 5 | 28 | 0 |
| King | 3 | 23 | 0 |
| Pittman | 4 | 20 | 0 |
| R. Johnson | 1 | 5 | 0 |
| Stecker | 1 | -2 | 0 |

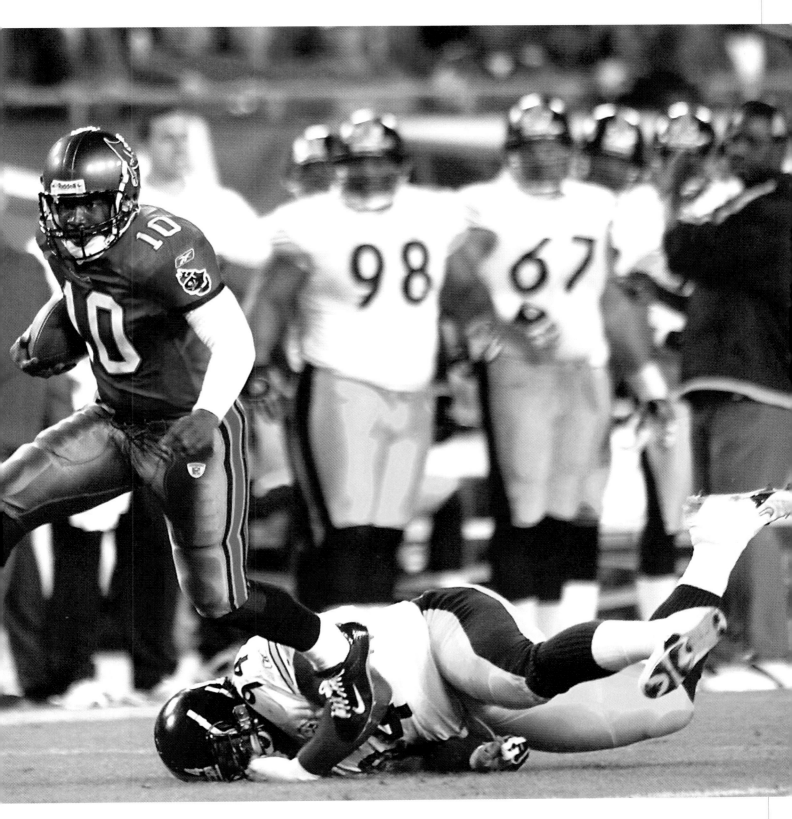

**ABOVE:** Shaun King of the Bucs scrambles for a first down over Rodney Bailey of the Steelers. John Raoux/Orlando Sentinel

# TAMPA BAY 15
## GAME SIXTEEN
## CHICAGO 0

# TAMPA BAY BANISHES COLD-WEATHER DEMONS

### BY CHRIS HARRY, ORLANDO SENTINEL

A cold day in central Illinois became the cold day in hell for the chill-challenged Tampa Bay Buccaneers.

Their hopes for a playoff bye seemingly left for dead, the Bucs gave new life to their postseason Sunday night, defeating the Chicago Bears and their cold-weather demons 15-0 before a crowd of 55,832 at the University of Illinois's Memorial Stadium.

Martin Gramatica kicked five field goals, backup quarterback Rob Johnson was cautiously effective and the league's top-ranked defense rang up its second shutout of the season to give the guys in pewter a belated Christmas gift that last week seemed unlikely.

In setting a franchise record for regular-season victories, the Bucs (12-4) finally won for the first time when the game-time temperature was 40 degrees or below; they had been 0-21 in such conditions. By snapping the cold streak, the Bucs guaranteed themselves a warm weekend at home in two weeks. That the win happened on the heels of last Monday night's embarrassing and decisive home loss against Pittsburgh made the fortuitous turn of events all the more satisfying.

"We got the abominable snowman off our backs," defensive tackle Warren Sapp said. "And the situation we let get away from us last week fell right back into our laps."

As the No. 2 seed in the NFC, Tampa Bay will be off next weekend, then host a game Jan. 11 or 12 against the highest-seeded survivor of next weekend's conference wild-card games. The worst remaining seed will go to Philadelphia.

"The bye week is huge," Bucs coach Jon Gruden said. "It's like winning a playoff game."

After the New York Jets blasted the Green Bay Packers 42-17 earlier in the day, the Bucs took the field knowing a victory over a four-win team would secure the No. 2 seed behind the Eagles.

What happened over the next three hours wasn't pretty (it often isn't with this bunch), but for a team with so much on the line—and with that icy 0-21 record and last week's punking by the Steelers as backdrops— aesthetics were irrelevant.

"You had a league full of teams not stepping up, so we felt like an opportunity was there for ourselves," said strong safety John Lynch, who along with his teammates watched the likes of the Miami Dolphins and New Orleans Saints blow chances to clinch playoff berths.

---

RIGHT: **Buccaneers kicker Martin Gramatica pats teammate Roman Oben on the helmet after one of Gramatica's field goals in the fourth quarter.**
M. Spencer Green, AP/Wide World Photos

ABOVE: Tampa Bay tight end Ken Dilger (85) gains yardage after a reception as Chicago's Brian Urlacher (54) and Jerry Azumah (23) take him down. Dilger caught three passes for 32 yards in the game.
Tom Roberts, AP/Wide World Photos

"We screwed it up last week. You can sulk about it or you can do something about it."

The Bucs chose the latter, but needed field goals from Gramatica of 30, 32, 33, 26 and 33 yards, the last three coming in the fourth quarter, to get it done.

"We held them to five field goals, but we couldn't get anything going on offense," Bears coach Dick Jauron said. "It was hard to do against this football team."

Henry Burris got the crowd excited with a couple of scrambles and one or two pass plays, but three of his four interceptions set up Tampa Bay field goals. He was intercepted three times in the fourth quarter, twice by cornerback Brian Kelly, and finished with just 78 yards passing before being benched late for the equally obscure Cory Sauter.

Tampa Bay's backup quarterback wasn't asked to do much. Johnson was sacked five times but was 16 of 25 for 134 yards without an interception or a fumble. He has started twice this season, and the offense hasn't scored a touchdown in either of the games. Both were wins, though.

The score was 6-0 until the fourth quarter when the Bucs put together a 15-play, 65-yard drive that ended with Gramatica's third field goal.

"In a game of backup quarterbacks, a two-possession lead is huge," said Gruden, who commended his players for seizing the cold moment and making history. "Hopefully, we can put some of these streaks to an end and maybe start some cold-weather victory streaks."

For the time being, his team will be more than content to play its next game at a warm-weather site. After all, the last (and only) time the Bucs had a first-round bye, they advanced to the NFC Championship Game after the 1999 season.

"I've taken this route before," Sapp said. "It's a good route."

RIGHT: Bears defender Phillip Daniels pursues Buccaneers quarterback Rob Johnson in the first quarter. Johnson completed just 16 of 25 pass attempts and was sacked five times.
AP Photo/M. Spencer Green

**"** In a game of backup quarterbacks, a two-possession lead is huge. Hopefully, we can put some of these streaks to an end and maybe start some cold-weather victory streaks. **"**

— Bucs coach Jon Gruden, commending his players for seizing the cold moment and making history

| | 1st | 2nd | 3rd | 4th | Final |
|---|---|---|---|---|---|
| Tampa Bay | 0 | 6 | 0 | 9 | 15 |
| Chicago | 0 | 0 | 0 | 0 | 0 |

## SCORING SUMMARY

| Qtr | Team | Play | | Time |
|---|---|---|---|---|
| 2nd | Buccaneers | FG | Gramatica 30-yd. field goal | 3:26 |
| 2nd | Buccaneers | FG | Gramatica 32-yd. field goal | 0:06 |
| 4th | Buccaneers | FG | Gramatica 33-yd. field goal | 13:16 |
| 4th | Buccaneers | FG | Gramatica 26-yd. field goal | 7:05 |
| 4th | Buccaneers | FG | Gramatica 33-yd. field goal | 3:14 |

## OFFENSE

### BUCCANEERS

| PASSING | COMP | ATT | YDS | TD | INT |
|---|---|---|---|---|---|
| R. Johnson | 16 | 25 | 134 | 0 | 0 |

| RECEIVING | REC | YDS | TD |
|---|---|---|---|
| K. Johnson | 5 | 41 | 0 |
| Dilger | 3 | 32 | 0 |
| Pittman | 2 | 28 | 0 |
| Jurevicius | 2 | 12 | 0 |
| McCardell | 2 | 11 | 0 |
| Dudley | 1 | 6 | 0 |
| Alstott | 1 | 4 | 0 |

| RUSHING | ATT | YDS | TD |
|---|---|---|---|
| Pittman | 21 | 90 | 0 |
| Alstott | 12 | 42 | 0 |
| R. Johnson | 3 | 29 | 0 |

### BEARS

| PASSING | COMP | ATT | YDS | TD | INT |
|---|---|---|---|---|---|
| Burris | 7 | 19 | 78 | 0 | 4 |
| Sauter | 6 | 9 | 59 | 0 | 0 |
| Booker | 0 | 1 | 0 | 0 | 0 |

| RECEIVING | REC | YDS | TD |
|---|---|---|---|
| Johnson | 1 | 31 | 0 |
| Gilmore | 1 | 30 | 0 |
| Merritt | 4 | 28 | 0 |
| White | 2 | 21 | 0 |
| Booker | 4 | 19 | 0 |
| Shelton | 1 | 8 | 0 |

| RUSHING | ATT | YDS | TD |
|---|---|---|---|
| Peterson | 7 | 42 | 0 |
| Johnson | 9 | 21 | 0 |
| Burris | 4 | 14 | 0 |
| Sauter | 2 | 8 | 0 |

**RIGHT: Tampa Bay's Michael Pittman rushes past Chicago's Brian Urlacher (54), Rosevelt Colvin (59) and Mike Brown (30) in the first quarter.**
Tom Roberts, AP/Wide World Photos

# WARREN

# SAPP

## The Mouth that Roared

ED HINTON, ORLANDO SENTINEL

**O**nce Warren Sapp had taken "the biggest stage I know," he wouldn't leave.

He shouted down the loudspeakers at Qualcomm Stadium on Super Bowl media day when they blared, "Attention media: Buccaneers media day is now over."

"I ain't goin' nowhere!" Sapp boomed. And kept talking.

After a while, an NFL publicist was sent to fetch him down. No luck. Then a Bucs PR guy was called in; maybe a homeboy could get his attention. Uh-uh.

Finally, from the media crowd that lingered around the talkingest tackle in the history of defensive football, the Bucs' publicist howled in agony, "You don't want to stay here all day, do you, Warren?"

"You gotta take me?" Sapp moaned. "Where I gotta go?"

Well, there was practice for the first Super Bowl the Tampa Bay franchise has ever been to.

"Two more minutes," Sapp pleaded. And continued, savoring every last syllable he could roll off his tongue. Even as he was led away, he stopped for a final soliloquy, three minutes with a Danish television crew.

Three extra sets of bleachers had been erected for the reporters and camera crews who deemed Warren Sapp at the Super Bowl to be a hotter attraction than Chris Rock in Vegas, and still Sapp's audience spilled over onto bleachers meant for Bucs quarterback Brad Johnson, and still it was jostling room only.

"It looks like a multitude of people, right here," Sapp said. "And we're in the middle of it. It's a feeding frenzy. It's a blast."

"It's my opportunity to say some lovely things and some crazy things," he said, then tightened up. "But I'm almost in awe just sitting here."

Then he repeated what had turned out to be his sparse mantra for the day: "Wow."

Was he simply speechless—for him, at least?

He nodded, laughed and said, "It's crazy. They talk about the thousands of credentials that go around the world and the people that'll be here. But . . . wow . . . I've been to back-to-back national championship games [at the University of Miami], but nothing like the Super Bowl. I'm a witness now."

Warren Sapp? A passive witness? This was so out of character, he had to be choking.

"I'm not crazy," Sapp had said upon his arrival in San Diego during Super Bowl week. "Make no mistake about it: I have a lot of confidence in this club. But until we go out here and work on this game plan and see what these guys [the Oakland Raiders] have to offer, I'm not about to say anything other than I'm just happy to be here."

Yet as the minutes of his long-awaited hour wound down, Sapp began to seize his moment, gather his game, hit his stride of eloquence.

Just a moment ago, to him, "We were at home playing San Francisco to get to Philly. Now we're here in the blink of an eye. In another blink of an eye I'll be looking up at a scoreboard at the end of 60 minutes to see if we are where we want to be.

"This thing will fly by. I was thinking back to when I'd just left Apopka High on my way to Miami to go to school and try to become something. Now here I am 12 years later, standing almost at that mountaintop. And it feels damn good."

It felt fabulous "to be in the company of a man worth $8 million and four draft picks," he said of Bucs coach Jon Gruden, and with this, the Sapp yapping hit full force.

"We paid a king's ransom for Gruden," he said. "But from where we sit right now, we didn't pay enough. We should have tossed in two more million to be where we are right now. He came in with direction and vision and put it right in front of us.

"He's always ready to go. He's the Energizer Bunny. You gotta be, to get up at 3:15 in the morning and come to work.

"The only thing he was about was winning the championship and winning it right now."

That meant everything to an eight-year defensive tackle who'd endured the rise from the Yucs to the Bucs.

"We were the laughingstock of the league for a long time. When you talk about turning around years and years and years of bad football, that takes a whole makeover. That's a big Mary Kay. I think we're the biggest Mary Kay you could find. From popsicle orange to this pewter we have on now, it's a wonderful feeling."

Finally, here at "The Greatest Show on Green Grass," as Sapp has renamed the Super Bowl, it was time to hit the bottom line.

In the Raiders and the Bucs, "We have the No. 1 offense against the No. 1 defense. Let's play.

"Ain't no talk gonna win this game."

Gary Bogdon/Orlando Sentinel

# SAN FRANCISCO 6
## DIVISION PLAYOFFS
# TAMPA BAY 31

# BUCS DOMINATE THE COMPETITION

## BY CHRIS HARRY, ORLANDO SENTINEL

The Tampa Bay Buccaneers have won postseason games before, but they've never looked as ready to play for a berth in their first Super Bowl as they did Sunday in overwhelming the San Francisco 49ers.

The trademark defense swarmed, the resurrected offense stormed and the combination warmed Raymond James Stadium to a fever pitch as the Bucs flogged the Niners 31-6 in an NFC divisional playoff game in front of a crazed sellout crowd of 65,599 that gave its team a wild send-off to destiny's doorstep.

"We put ourselves in the position that everybody wants to be in," Tampa Bay defensive end Simeon Rice said. "And if we didn't want it, we'd have gone out and lost."

Instead, the Bucs (13-4) put together their most dominant playoff victory in the franchise's 27-season history and with it advanced to the NFC championship game, where they'll face their No. 1 nemesis, the Philadelphia Eagles (13-4), Sunday at 3:00 p.m.

The winner will move on to Super Bowl XXXVII at San Diego.

"We've got 60 minutes to go to get to the game that we've all dreamed about since childhood," said Tampa Bay coach Jon Gruden, whose team has lost four straight to the Eagles, including a 20-10 defeat on Oct. 20. "I'm so proud of what these guys have accomplished, but we're not satisfied yet. We've got some work to do still."

Quarterback Brad Johnson, who watched from the sideline with a sore back as the offense struggled in the final two regular-season games, returned to the lineup and showed why he's the team's most valuable player on offense. Johnson passed for 196 yards and two touchdowns, leading a unit that cranked out 329 yards and converted 10 of 17 third-down opportunities.

Johnson engineered four touchdown drives in the first half alone, including touchdown strikes of 20 yards to wideout Joe Jurevicius and 12 to tight end Rickey Dudley. Fullback Mike Alstott scored the other two on short runs.

"If you look at us from the midseason on, that's where we really took off," Johnson said of an offense that looks nothing like those of the Tony Dungy years. "Everyone talks about the defense, but I think we've earned our respect."

Johnson certainly has. In the second half, 49ers linebacker Derek Smith put a finger through Johnson's facemask trying to make a tackle. The quarterback suffered a cut to his forehead and had to leave the game, blood covering his face, and headed for the locker room to get stitched.

He came back to the roar of the crowd.

---

**RIGHT: Tampa Bay quarterback Brad Johnson laughs with coach Jon Gruden during the final moments of the Buccaneers' 31-6 victory over the '49ers.**
John Raoux/Orlando Sentinel

**ABOVE: Tampa Bay's Michael Pittman runs for yardage against the 49ers. Pittman gained 41 yards on 17 carries for the Buccaneers.** John Raoux/Orlando Sentinel

"Who wouldn't want to play for a guy like that?" offensive guard Cosey Coleman asked.

And who wouldn't want the Tampa Bay defense on its side? The Bucs stymied the 49ers (11-7) a week after they cranked out 458 yards and 39 points in an epic comeback against the New York Giants. Down 28-6, the Niners had no choice but to pass almost exclusively, which played into the belly of the Bucs' beast.

The Niners finished with a season-low 228 yards and went without a touchdown for the first time in 26 playoff games, dating to the 1986 season.

"We know our defense is playing great," Tampa Bay receiver Keenan McCardell said.

"You saw what kind of team we can be when the offense does its part and puts some points on the board."

Unlike the game against the Giants, San Francisco quarterback Jeff Garcia was completely thrown out of his rhythm and never got star wideout Terrell Owens—he of the nine catches, 177 yards and two touchdowns a week earlier—into any kind of a flow.

Garcia finished 22 of 41 for 193 yards and was intercepted three times, part of five turnovers forced by the relentless Bucs defense.

"When they get ahead, that defense gets in its track stances," 49ers coach Steve Mariucci said.

The visitors had a shot to jump ahead early when safety John Keith intercepted Johnson on the game's first series, giving San Francisco a first down at the

Tampa Bay 40. Right then, the Bucs let Garcia know how it was going to be, forcing a three and out and subsequent punt.

With that, the Bucs marched 74 yards in 12 plays, converting a trio of third downs (one by penalty) along the way. Alstott's two-yard burst not only put the home team up 7-0 at 6:34 of the first quarter, but also represented the first postseason touchdown for the club since the 1999 season.

"Jon has an attack that's working right now," defensive tackle Warren Sapp said. "Once we got up, it was on us."

In the second quarter, Johnson drove the Bucs to three touchdowns in four possessions, against one Jeff Chandler field goal, and went to the locker room leading 28-6.

The second half was more of the first. Garcia had no chance.

"We wanted to get pressure, make the pocket uncomfortable and contain him on the scrambles," said linebacker Derrick Brooks, who four days earlier was named NFL Defensive Player of the Year.

"In other words, we played our defense. It wasn't any magic formula. We've been doing it for eight years now."

In that time, the Bucs have been this close to the grand prize only once before. They came within four minutes of the Super Bowl three years ago but couldn't sniff it the two years that followed, losing twice in humbling postseason fashion—21-3 in 2000 and 31-9 last season—on the road.

At Philadelphia.

"Like Jon says, we'll play anyone anywhere," cornerback Ronde Barber said. "We'll see next week what our fortunes hold, but I can't think of a better place to go try to win an NFC championship."

Or a better time.

**RIGHT: Buccaneers fans celebrate their team's first touchdown of the day, a two-yard run by Mike Alstott.** John Raoux/Orlando Sentinel

| | 1st | 2nd | 3rd | 4th | Final |
|---|---|---|---|---|---|
| San Francisco | 3 | 3 | 0 | 0 | 6 |
| Tampa Bay | 7 | 21 | 3 | 0 | 31 |

## SCORING SUMMARY

| Qtr | Team | Play | | Time |
|---|---|---|---|---|
| 1st | Buccaneers | TD | Alstott 2-yd. run (Gramatica kick) | 6:34 |
| 1st | 49ers | FG | Chandler 24-yd. field goal | 0:22 |
| 2nd | Buccaneers | TD | Jurevicius 20-yd. pass from B. Johnson (Gramatica kick) | 9:35 |
| 2nd | 49ers | FG | Chandler 40-yd. field goal | 8:36 |
| 2nd | Buccaneers | TD | Dudley 12-yd. pass from B. Johnson (Gramatica kick) | 7:31 |
| 2nd | Buccaneers | TD | Alstott 2-yd. run (Gramatica kick) | 0:55 |
| 3rd | Buccaneers | FG | Gramatica 19-yd. field goal | 8:33 |

## OFFENSE

### 49ERS

| PASSING | COMP | ATT | YDS | TD | INT |
|---|---|---|---|---|---|
| Garcia | 22 | 41 | 193 | 0 | 3 |

| RECEIVING | REC | YDS | TD |
|---|---|---|---|
| Streets | 5 | 62 | 0 |
| Owens | 4 | 35 | 0 |
| Hearst | 4 | 29 | 0 |
| Wilson | 1 | 22 | 0 |
| Stokes | 3 | 20 | 0 |
| Beasley | 2 | 15 | 0 |
| Johnson | 2 | 17 | 0 |
| Barlow | 1 | 3 | 0 |

| RUSHING | ATT | YDS | TD |
|---|---|---|---|
| Hearst | 10 | 55 | 0 |
| Barlow | 3 | 7 | 0 |

### BUCCANEERS

| PASSING | COMP | ATT | YDS | TD | INT |
|---|---|---|---|---|---|
| B. Johnson | 15 | 31 | 196 | 2 | 1 |
| R. Johnson | 1 | 1 | 21 | 0 | 0 |

| RECEIVING | REC | YDS | TD |
|---|---|---|---|
| K. Johnson | 5 | 85 | 0 |
| Jurevicius | 3 | 48 | 1 |
| Dilger | 3 | 35 | 0 |
| Alstott | 3 | 27 | 0 |
| Dudley | 1 | 12 | 1 |
| Pittman | 1 | 10 | 0 |

| RUSHING | ATT | YDS | TD |
|---|---|---|---|
| Alstott | 17 | 60 | 2 |
| Pittman | 17 | 41 | 0 |
| Stecker | 2 | 8 | 0 |
| R. Johnson | 1 | 7 | 0 |
| B. Johnson | 1 | 5 | 0 |

**ABOVE: Mike Alstott (40) celebrates with Warren Sapp after Alstott scored a first-quarter touchdown to give the Buccaneers a 7-0 lead. Sapp, a Pro Bowl defensive tackle, lined up with the offense on the play.** John Raoux/Orlando Sentinel

## TAMPA BAY 27
### NFC CHAMPIONSHIP
## PHILADELPHIA 10

# BUCS PUNCH TICKET TO SUPER BOWL

**BY CHRIS HARRY, ORLANDO SENTINEL**

It started, fittingly, in Celebration last July.

And now the season just might end in one.

Veterans Stadium isn't due to be torn down until later this year, but the Tampa Bay Buccaneers commenced with the destruction Sunday by dismantling the Philadelphia Eagles and their hostile home crowd with a 27-10 rout in the NFC Championship Game before a stunned and silenced throng of 66,713.

Playing in cold weather, on the road and against their biggest nemesis of the last two seasons, the Bucs stared down and then conquered all their demons in resounding fashion to clinch the first Super Bowl berth in the franchise's 27-year history.

Tampa Bay (14-4) will face the AFC champion Oakland Raiders (13-5) in Super Bowl XXXVII in San Diego next Sunday night in a game that will pit Bucs coach Jon Gruden against the team he coached the previous four seasons.

Last February, Tampa Bay owner Malcolm Glazer gave his sons the OK to send two first-round draft picks, two second-round picks and $8 million to tear Gruden from the final year of his Oakland contract.

Today, it looks like a bargain.

"We beat a great football team," Gruden said in becoming the team's first coach in seven tries to win a road playoff game.""It's kind of like that movie, *The Wizard of Oz*. Ding-dong, the witch is dead! We won a cold game, a road playoff game and we scored a touchdown here at the Vet. So, hopefully, some of those stories will go away."

As the Vet's clock ticked off the final seconds, the Bucs strutted the sidelines and mocked the smattering of Philly fans who stuck around to wallow in their misery. Waving team logo flags and wearing championship hats, Tampa Bay players rejoiced in their finest hour.

"I don't know whether to scream, laugh or cry," wide receiver Keyshawn Johnson shouted.

"Do 'em all," defensive end Simeon Rice said.

He did. They all did.

Amid the euphoria, the team's defining triumvirate—linebacker Derrick Brooks, defensive tackle Warren Sapp and strong safety John Lynch, a combined 26 years and 17 Pro Bowls in the organization—embraced for what had to be the most satisfying moment of their sensational careers. It was here, after all, that the last two Tampa Bay seasons ended with humiliating playoff defeats, the most recent leading to the firing of beloved former coach Tony Dungy.

"I came to the Bucs when we were the Yuks," said Lynch, the most tenured Tampa Bay player at 10 seasons.

"To go .500 was a big deal. We got it to where we were a perennial playoff team, but that wasn't good enough. We kept working toward that prize."

**RIGHT: Tampa Bay's Ken Dilger breaks a tackle by Ike Reese of the Eagles in the second half.**
Shoun A. Hill/Orlando Sentinel

ABOVE: **Buccaneers ballcarrier Aaron Stecker tries to get through the Eagle defense as he is tackled by the Eagles' Carlos Emmons.** John Raoux/Orlando Sentinel

Said Sapp: "Tell 'em back home to pack their bags for California."

"I wish the million or so people of Tampa Bay could have been here to see this," said Brooks, the NFL's 2002 Defensive Player of the Year. "But they saw it through our eyes."

There was quarterback Brad Johnson, whom the Eagles treated like a heavy bag the last two times, picking apart a secondary containing three Pro Bowlers while executing a masterful Gruden game plan. Johnson completed 20 of 33 passes for 259 yards, including a nine-yard touchdown strike to Keyshawn Johnson that came with 2:28 to go in the first half and gave the Bucs the lead for good.

There was a much-maligned offensive line—whose members watched ESPN analyst Steve Young refer to them as "below average" earlier in the day—neutralizing an Eagles defense that led the league in sacks. Brad Johnson wasn't sacked.

And then there was the defense that has meant everything to the organization since joining the league's elite seven years ago.

Now they're on the verge of joining the NFL's all-time elite.

"Every week we go out and say we have to outplay our opponent's defense, but all we heard all week was how great the Eagles were," said cornerback Ronde Barber, whose 92-yard interception return for a late touchdown sealed the deal. "It didn't matter to us. We know we're the best, and we prove it every week."

"Training camp seems like an eternity ago," said Bucs offensive tackle Roman Oben, who signed a free-agent deal with the team barely a month before the Bucs reported to the Celebration Hotel for camp at Disney's Wide World of Sports. "At the same time, I don't think it's all hit me yet."

Maybe there's a reason for that.

"We've done something special," said running back Mike Alstott, one of five current Bucs who once donned those hideous Creamsicle orange uniforms. "I feel great for all the people back in Tampa who supported us through all those tough years. This one is for them. They can enjoy it this week."

He nodded.

"But we've got work to do."

**ABOVE:** Buccaneers quarterback Brad Johnson and teammate Roman Oben celebrate Tampa Bay's first touchdown. Gary W. Green/Orlando Sentinel

**ABOVE:** Tampa Bay defenders Shelton Quarles (53) and Warren Sapp (99) sandwich Eagles running back Dorsey Levens in the second half.
Shoun A. Hill/Orlando Sentinel

**RIGHT:** Eagles quarterback Donovan NcNabb throws off his back foot to avoid the pressure put on by Warren Sapp and the rest of the Bucs defense. Shoun A. Hill/ Orlando Sentinel

| | 1st | 2nd | 3rd | 4th | Final |
|---|---|---|---|---|---|
| New Orleans | 10 | 7 | 3 | 7 | 27 |
| Tampa Bay | 7 | 3 | 0 | 0 | 10 |

## SCORING SUMMARY

| Qtr | Team | Play | | Time |
|---|---|---|---|---|
| 1st | Eagles | TD | Staley 20-yd. run (Akers kick) | 14:15 |
| 1st | Buccaneers | FG | Gramatica 48-yd. field goal | 10:01 |
| 1st | Buccaneers | TD | Alstott 1-yd. run (Gramatica kick) | 0:43 |
| 2nd | Eagles | FG | Akers 30-yd. field goal | 8:06 |
| 2nd | Buccaneers | TD | K. Johnson 9-yd. pass from B. Johnson (Gramatica kick) | 2:31 |
| 3rd | Buccaneers | FG | Gramatica 27-yd. field goal | 1:06 |
| 4th | Buccaneers | TD | Barber 92-yd. interception return (Gramatica kick) | 3:27 |

## OFFENSE

### BUCCANEERS

| PASSING | COMP | ATT | YDS | TD | INT |
|---|---|---|---|---|---|
| B. Johnson | 20 | 33 | 259 | 1 | 11 |

| RECEIVING | REC | YDS | TD |
|---|---|---|---|
| Jurevicius | 1 | 71 | 0 |
| Pittman | 5 | 53 | 0 |
| Dilger | 3 | 41 | 0 |
| K. Johnson | 3 | 40 | 1 |
| McCardell | 5 | 37 | 0 |
| Dudley | 1 | 7 | 0 |
| Williams | 1 | 7 | 0 |
| Stecker | 1 | 3 | 00 |

| RUSHING | ATT | YDS | TD |
|---|---|---|---|
| McAAlstott | 17 | 25 | 1 |
| Pittman | 8 | 17 | 0 |
| Stecker | 1 | 9 | 0 |
| B. Johnson | 6 | -2 | 0 |

### EAGLES

| PASSING | COMP | ATT | YDS | TD | INT |
|---|---|---|---|---|---|
| McNabb | 26 | 49 | 243 | 0 | 1 |

| RECEIVING | REC | YDS | TD |
|---|---|---|---|
| KFreeman | 5 | 66 | 0 |
| Lewis | 6 | 65 | 0 |
| Pinkston | 3 | 51 | 0 |
| Staley | 6 | 26 | 0 |
| Thrash | 4 | 23 | 0 |
| Westbrook | 1 | 8 | 0 |
| Martin | 1 | 4 | 0 |

| RUSHING | ATT | YDS | TD |
|---|---|---|---|
| Staley | 13 | 58 | 1 |
| McNabb | 3 | 17 | 0 |
| Westbrook | 2 | 5 | 0 |
| Levens | 3 | 0 | 0 |

RIGHT: Tampa Bay's Dwight Smith (left) celebrates with teammate Ronde Barber (20) after Barber returned an interception for a fourth-quarter touchdown. Gary W. Green/ Orlando Sentinel

CAUTION 17° WIND CHILL

HOWELL 38

**ABOVE:** Eagles and Bucs fans alike cheer Tampa Bay players—including safety John Howell— as they leave the stadium. John Raoux/Orlando Sentinel

**RIGHT:** Buccaneer fans cheer the team as the players leave Raymond James Stadium in Tampa for San Diego and Super Bowl XXXVII. Joe Burbank/Orlando Sentinel

**❝ I wish the million or so people of Tampa Bay could have been here to see this. But they saw it through our eyes. ❞**

**—Derrick Brooks, NFL 2002 Defensive Player of the Year**

**LEFT:** Tampa Bay's Simeon Rice celebrates the Buccaneers' 27-10 win over the Philadelphia Eagles in the NFC Championship Game at Veterans Stadium.

Gary W. Green/Orlando Sentinel

# RAIDERS 21

## SUPER BOWL XXXVII

# TAMPA BAY 48

# CHAMPS!

## BY CHRIS HARRY, ORLANDO SENTINEL

The Oakland Raiders can have those two first-round picks, two second-rounders and $8 million.

The Tampa Bay Buccaneers have a world championship. And Jon Gruden got it for them at his former team's expense.

Those seemingly endless years of futility and aggravating postseason exits of recent years disappeared into the California night Sunday as the Bucs obliterated the Oakland Raiders 48-21 to capture their first NFL title in a Super Bowl XXXVII blowout before 67,603 at Qualcomm Stadium.

Three interception returns for touchdowns—all in the second half—put a fitting exclamation point on a game that was billed as a matchup between Oakland and its top-ranked offense against Tampa Bay and its No. 1 defense.

The matchup was a mismatch, almost as lopsided as the Bucs' edge in the controversial trade of 11 months ago that pried Gruden from the final year of his contract with the Raiders and brought him to Tampa with one goal in mind.

To raise the Lombardi Trophy.

So there Gruden was, alongside team owner Malcolm Glazer, basking in a championship realized. It was a vision that was the goal from the minute the season officially convened last July 28 at—get this—the Celebration Hotel for training camp at Disney's Wide World of Sports.

"I knew I was coming into a sensitive situation," said an emotional Gruden, who replaced the beloved Tony Dungy, fired despite leading the team to four playoff appearances in six seasons. "Tony Dungy did a great job. I reaped a lot of his benefits. But I'm the coach of the Tampa Bay Buccaneers, I'm wearing the hat of a world champion, and I'm going to enjoy it."

He wasn't alone. This one was for the orange uniforms and Buccaneer Bruce; for Lee Roy Selmon and Doug Williams; for the long-suffering faithful of what once was mocked as the worst organization in professional sports; for Warren Sapp, Derrick Brooks and John Lynch.

"I've never done this before," said Lynch, the Buc with the most tenure at 10 years. "It feels sweet, but I have to believe it's even sweeter after going through all the things we've been through."

Bringing it together was Gruden, who built Oakland into a powerhouse in four seasons there (1998-2001) before jumping coasts last winter.

"You knew there was something special about him from day one," Bucs quarterback Brad Johnson said. "The guy is contagious, and I love coming to work and dealing with him every day and just learning from the guy."

RIGHT: **Dexter Jackson heads up-field after his second interception against the Raiders in the game.**
Shoun A. Hill/Orlando Sentinel

ABOVE: **Simeon Rice celebrates with Greg Spires after a sack on Raiders quarterback Rich Gannon. Rice sacked Gannon twice in the game.** Gary W. Green/Orlando Sentinel

Despite falling behind by a field goal in the opening minutes, the Bucs (15-4) stormed to 34 unanswered points.

It took an official's reversal for a touchdown, a couple of special-teams blunders and an oh-by-the-way touchdown pass to the incomparable Jerry Rice, 40, to pull the Raiders (13-6) within 34-21 late in the fourth quarter and make the game appear remotely competitive. The look was deceiving.

"What comeback?" asked Sapp, the heart of a defensive front that put the clamps on NFL Most Valuable Player Rich Gannon and the explosive Raiders, holding them to a mere 269 yards and just 19 rushing. "A couple special-teams screw-ups and a fluke over-the-top pass? There wasn't gonna be any comeback."

No image could have been as appropriate as the sight of Brooks—the linebacker, leader and NFL's Defensive Player of the Year—intercepting Gannon and racing 44 yards for a touchdown with 1:18 left to set off a celebration 27 years in the making. And as if that wasn't good enough, there went nickel back Dwight Smith five plays later with his second interception and touchdown return with two seconds to go, giving the Bucs the fourth highest point total ever in a Super Bowl.

"We set the momentum early and held it for the entire game," Brooks said.

Tampa Bay quarterback Brad Johnson wasn't sharp early, but he found his touch in the second quarter. Johnson passed for 215 yards and two short touchdowns to Keenan McCardell, while getting a surprising lift from

**ABOVE: Keenan McCardell celebrates with Keshawn Johnson after catching one of his two touchdown receptions on the day.** Gary W. Green/Orlando Sentinel

a running game—150 yards, with a season-high 124 from tailback Michael Pittman—that was invisible most of the year. The Bucs finished with 365 total yards.

But as impressive a display as the offense put on, it was the Tampa Bay defense—of course—that wrote the script by flushing, flustering and frustrating Gannon.

The game tape will reveal that the Bucs were a factor. Free safety Dexter Jackson, voted the game's Most Valuable Player, intercepted Gannon twice in a first half, in which the high-powered Raiders totaled just 62 yards (second fewest in Super Bowl history) and fell behind 20-3.

The Raiders managed to pull within 34-21. They figured they had hope. Against the Bucs' defense, though, it was hopeless.

Those two touchdowns Oakland needed in the final minutes instead were scored by Tampa Bay as Gruden—the man who'd sunk his life into both these teams the past five years—pumped his fist in triumph on the sideline.

What a year it was.

|  | 1st | 2nd | 3rd | 4th | Final |
|---|---|---|---|---|---|
| Oakland | 3 | 0 | 6 | 12 | **21** |
| Tampa Bay | 3 | 17 | 14 | 14 | **48** |

## SCORING SUMMARY

| Qtr | Team | Play | | Time |
|---|---|---|---|---|
| 1st | Raiders | FG | Janikowski 40-yd. field goal | 4:20 |
| 1st | Buccaneers | FG | Gramatica 24-yd. field goal | 7:09 |
| 2nd | Buccaneers | FG | Gramatica 43-yd. field goal | 3:44 |
| 2nd | Buccaneers | TD | Alstott 2-yd. run (Gramatica kick) | 8:36 |
| 2nd | Buccaneers | TD | McCardell 5-yd. pass from B. Johnson (Gramatica kick) | 14:30 |
| 3rd | Buccaneers | TD | McCardell 8-yd. pass from B. Johnson (Gramatica kick) | 9:30 |
| 3rd | Buccaneers | TD | D. Smith 44-yd. interception return (Gramatica kick) | 10:13 |
| 3rd | Raiders | TD | Porter 39-yd. pass from Gannon (2-pt. conv. failed) | 12:46 |
| 4th | Raiders | TD | Johnson 13-yd. blocked punt return (2-pt. conv. failed) | 0:44 |
| 4th | Raiders | TD | Rice 48-yd. pass from Gannon (2-pt. conv. failed) | 8:54 |
| 4th | Buccaneers | TD | Brooks 44-yd. interception return (Gramatica kick) | 13:42 |
| 4th | Buccaneers | TD | D. Smith 50-yd. interception return (Gramatica kick) | 14:58 |

## OFFENSE

### RAIDERS

| PASSING | COMP | ATT | YDS | TD | INT |
|---|---|---|---|---|---|
| Gannon | 24 | 44 | 272 | 2 | 5 |

| RECEIVING | REC | YDS | TD |
|---|---|---|---|
| Rice | 5 | 77 | 1 |
| Porter | 4 | 62 | 1 |
| Jolley | 5 | 59 | 0 |
| Garner | 7 | 51 | 0 |
| Brown | 1 | 9 | 0 |
| Wheatley | 1 | 7 | 0 |
| Ritchie | 1 | 7 | 0 |

| RUSHING | ATT | YDS | TD |
|---|---|---|---|
| Garner | 7 | 10 | 0 |
| Crockett | 2 | 6 | 0 |
| Gannon | 2 | 3 | 0 |

### BUCCANEERS

| PASSING | COMP | ATT | YDS | TD | INT |
|---|---|---|---|---|---|
| B. Johnson | 18 | 34 | 215 | 2 | 1 |

| RECEIVING | REC | YDS | TD |
|---|---|---|---|
| Jurevicius | 4 | 78 | 0 |
| K. Johnson | 6 | 69 | 0 |
| Alstott | 5 | 43 | 0 |
| McCardell | 2 | 13 | 2 |
| Dilger | 1 | 12 | 0 |

| RUSHING | ATT | YDS | TD |
|---|---|---|---|
| Pittman | 29 | 124 | 0 |
| Alstott | 10 | 15 | 1 |
| B. Johnson | 1 | 10 | 0 |
| McCardell | 1 | 1 | 0 |
| Dilger | 1 | 0 | 0 |

**RIGHT: Keenan McCardell hauls in a TD pass over Raiders cornerback Charles Woodson.**
Gary W. Green/Orlando Sentinel

**❝ You knew there was something special about him from day one. The guy is contagious, and I love coming to work and dealing with him every day and just learning from the guy. ❞**

—Bucs quarterback
Brad Johnson on
Bucs coach
Jon Gruden

RIGHT: Bucs quarterback Brad Johnson holds his son Max as they listen to the MVP announcement after the game.
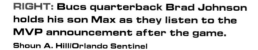
Shoun A. Hill/Orlando Sentinel

# MEGA-BUCS!

**BY DAVID WHITLEY, ORLANDO SENTINEL**

Stop the world. The Oakland Raiders want to get off. And guess who is sitting on top of it this morning?

Pinch yourself, get out the scissors, snip out these paragraphs. You might want to show them one day to your great-grandkids.

The Tampa Bay Buccaneers are world champions.

They didn't just win Super Bowl XXXVII on Sunday. They demolished the Raiders 48-21, emphatically burying the ghosts of their laughingstock past.

"By God, this is Tampa Bay's night," Coach Jon Gruden said. "We're Super Bowl champions."

They burst to a 34-3 lead, then fooled around just long enough to keep the world's TV sets tuned in. The Bucs then zipped away behind an avalanche of defensive points. The final exclamation point came when Dwight Smith returned an interception for a touchdown with two seconds left.

Gruden started dancing on the sideline, cannons full of confetti exploded, and Malcolm Glazer couldn't get his hands on the Super Bowl trophy quickly enough. The man with the funny beard bought the Bucs eight years ago and bankrolled them back from the dead.

"If you haven't heard about the Buccaneers, you heard about them today," Glazer said.

Until a couple of years ago, most of what you heard about the Bucs came in the form of a creamsicle-colored punch line. For sports fans, Tampa Bay's victory in front of 67,603 at Qualcomm Stadium was like watching Mr. Ed win the Kentucky Derby.

"It's hard to put into words right now," safety John Lynch said. "Having gone through what we've gone through in Tampa, to have been through so many tough times, it's the best."

He wasn't the only one having vocabulary trouble. "I can't explain it," Oakland owner Al Davis said. "I have no words."

Neither did the Raider Nation, that amalgam of freak-show characters that follows Oakland. The Darth Vader look-alikes will need a little nation-building after Sunday. But that job can't compare to the monumental task of raising the Bucs' ship from the mud of history.

In that context, Sunday's news ranks somewhere between man biting dog and Iraq freezing over. Or imagine the ugliest kid in high school showing up at the 20-year class reunion with Catherine Zeta-Jones on his arm.

Could these Bucs be the descendants of 0-26, Hugh Culverhouse and Bucco Bruce?

Bruce was the original mascot, the one with the permanent wink and the feather in his hat. Feathers aren't usually the preferred fashion statement in the macho NFL, and that wink became an acknowledgment that the joke would inevitably be on the fans.

This was the team that lost its first 26 games. This was the team that made players buy drinks out of the soda machine after practices. This was the team whose front office seemed to be occupied by the Marx Brothers.

It could all be summed up in the immortal quip from the original coach, John McKay, when he was asked what he thought of his team's execution after yet another loss.

"I'm in favor of it," McKay said.

John Madden reminded viewers of that comment Sunday night, then he pondered what McKay, Bill Parcells and Tony Dungy were thinking. Considering that McKay died last year, we'll just assume he was smiling down from that great skybox in the sky.

Dungy built the defense and finally instilled some pride in the franchise.

**ABOVE:** Bucs Coach Jon Gruden celebrates his team's Super Bowl victory. At age 39, Gruden became the youngest head coach to ever win a Super Bowl championship.

Gary W. Green/Orlando Sentinel

ABOVE: Warren Sapp celebrates the Bucs' Super Bowl win. Gary W. Green/Orlando Sentinel

If only the Bucs could have remembered how to score under Dungy, he might not have been fired after last season. The franchise temporarily reverted to Culverhouse form, trying to hire Parcells and then denying they'd ever heard of him.

In what now must rank as one of the great face-saving moves in sports history, the Parcells fiasco led to the hiring of Gruden. It cost the Bucs four prized draft picks and $8 million, but there wasn't a person within 100 miles of Qualcomm Stadium who didn't think it was worth it Sunday night.

"He came from heaven," Glazer said. "And he brought us heaven."

The final step was easier than almost everyone expected. The high-powered Raiders were four-point favorites, but Tampa Bay's defense easily handled the No. 1 offense in the NFL. The only suspense came after a couple of long touchdowns cut the Bucs' lead to 34-21.

ABC's Al Michaels even pondered whether he would have to dust off his famous "Do You Believe In Miracles?" line.

He didn't.

"The whole world saw it, almost a billion people," defensive end Simeon Rice said. "They probably saw it in Bangladesh."

People from Bangladesh to Brandon probably are pinching themselves.

The Bucs are Super Bowl champs.

Believe in miracles.

---

RIGHT: Tampa fans cheer their team after the Bucs routed the Raiders, 48-21, in the Super Bowl .
Gary W. Green/Orlando Sentinel

# "THANK YOU' GLAZERS, RICH, TONY & JON

# JACKSON NAMED SUPER BOWL MVP

**BY ED HINTON, ORLANDO SENTINEL**

Bucs safety Dexter Jackson was named the most valuable player of Super Bowl XXXVII for two interceptions in the first 20 minutes of the game that reduced Raiders quarterback Rich Gannon into a frustrated, grumbling, finger-pointing case of nerves.

That opened the floodgate for an onslaught that left the Bucs with more candidates for MVP than the Democrats have for president, and Gannon was intercepted a total of five times.

"People kept asking me how good this defense is," Jackson said, clutching the MVP trophy. "I said we'd have to play the No. 1 offense to see. Now I can say it's a great defense."

"When you're the No. 1 offense," Jackson said of the Raiders, "you think you can pass on anybody—even the No. 1 defense. They know now that our speed is for real."

Of being picked as MVP from the herd of standouts, "I am surprised," Jackson said. "It was just about opportunities tonight, being in the right place at the right time. They threw the ball my way, and I made the right plays."

If the Bucs' defensive front had more notoriety than the secondary, that was because, Jackson said, "During the season, people didn't challenge our defense downfield.

"Gannon tried to make some plays and threw the ball downfield. I just tried to break on the ball and capitalize."

After the two interceptions, Jackson said, "We could see Gannon getting frustrated. I saw Gannon start fussing at people. When you start pointing at people and fussing at them for being out of position, telling them it was their fault, you're frustrated."

Then they saw in Gannon the sure symptom in a quarterback that signals a fully discombobulated offense. "He was moving his feet a lot faster than normal," Jackson said. "He had what we call happy feet. He wasn't staying in the pocket real well. He was always on the run, trying to make something happen. We made him move his feet and throw bad passes."

Jackson returned his first interception nine yards to the Tampa Bay 49. From there the Bucs' offense moved into position for Martin Gramatica's 43-yard field goal that made it 6-3. Tampa never trailed after that.

Jackson's strongest interception return was the second one, 25 yards to the Oakland 45-yard line. The Bucs' offense couldn't quite capitalize directly, going three and out on the next possession, but Tom Tupa's punt backed the Raiders up to their own 11.

And that set the stage for the sack of Gannon at his 10, the Oakland punt and Williams's return to the Oakland 27. Four plays later, Mike Alstott banged in from two yards out for the Bucs' first touchdown, making it 13-3 and sending silver helmets visibly drooping on the field and the sidelines.

Because Jackson's early interceptions hadn't gone for touchdowns, and Smith's two interceptions had (though late), "I share [the MVP] award with Dwight Smith," Jackson said. "I share it with the whole secondary and the team. But back to the secondary . . .

"We felt like we were an overlooked unit. We had the No. 1 pass defense this year, and nobody ever gave us credit.

"How good is this defense?

"We're the champions. That's how good."

# BUCCANEERS' REGULAR SEASON STATISTICS

## OFFENSE

### PASSING

| Player | Att | Comp | Pct | Yds | TD | Int |
|---|---|---|---|---|---|---|
| B. Johnson | 451 | 281 | 62.3 | 3049 | 22 | 6 |
| R. Johnson | 88 | 57 | 64.8 | 536 | 1 | 2 |
| King | 27 | 10 | 37.0 | 80 | 0 | 1 |
| Tupa | 1 | 0 | 0 | 0 | 0 | 1 |

### RECEIVING

| Player | Rec | Yds | Avg | TD |
|---|---|---|---|---|
| K. Johnson | 76 | 1088 | 14.3 | 5 |
| McCardell | 61 | 670 | 11.0 | 6 |
| Pittman | 59 | 477 | 8.1 | 0 |
| Jurevicius | 37 | 423 | 11.4 | 4 |
| Dilger | 34 | 329 | 9.7 | 2 |
| Alstott | 35 | 242 | 6.9 | 2 |
| Dudley | 16 | 192 | 12.0 | 3 |
| Williams | 7 | 77 | 11.0 | 1 |
| Stecker | 13 | 69 | 5.3 | 0 |
| Cook | 4 | 43 | 10.8 | 0 |
| Yoder | 2 | 26 | 13.0 | 0 |
| Barlow | 3 | 23 | 7.7 | 0 |
| Stephens | 1 | 6 | 6.0 | 0 |

### RUSHING

| Player | Att | Yds | Avg | TD |
|---|---|---|---|---|
| Pittman | 204 | 718 | 3.5 | 1 |
| Alstott | 146 | 548 | 3.8 | 5 |
| Stecker | 28 | 174 | 6.2 | 0 |
| R. Johnson | 14 | 73 | 5.2 | 0 |
| B. Johnson | 13 | 30 | 2.3 | 0 |
| King | 4 | 25 | 6.3 | 0 |
| McCardell | 1 | 3 | 3.0 | 0 |
| Williams | 3 | -5 | -1.7 | 0 |
| Tupa | 1 | -9 | -9.0 | 0 |

## SPECIAL TEAMS

### FIELD GOALS

| Player | 1-19 | 20-29 | 30-39 | 40-49 | 50+ |
|---|---|---|---|---|---|
| Gramatica | 0/0 | 7/8 | 14/15 | 6/10 | 5/6 |

### PUNTING

| Player | No | Avg | Inside 20 |
|---|---|---|---|
| Tupa | 90 | 42.8 | 30 |
| Gramatica | 1 | 23.0 | 1 |

### PUNT RETURNS

| Player | No | FC | Yds | Avg | TD |
|---|---|---|---|---|---|
| Williams | 43 | 20 | 410 | 9.5 | 1 |
| Jackson | 1 | 0 | 20 | 20.0 | 0 |

### KICKOFF RETURNS

| Player | No | Yds | Avg | TD |
|---|---|---|---|---|
| Stecker | 37 | 934 | 25.2 | 0 |
| Smith | 4 | 93 | 23.3 | 0 |
| Williams | 3 | 49 | 16.3 | 0 |
| Yoder | 1 | 9 | 9.0 | 0 |

# DEFENSE

## TACKLES

| Player | No | Solo | Ast |
|---|---|---|---|
| Brooks | 87.0 | 70 | 30 |
| Quarles | 74.0 | 59 | 39 |
| Barber | 68.0 | 48 | 11 |
| Kelly | 57.0 | 47 | 8 |
| Jackson | 56.0 | 45 | 15 |
| Singleton | 43.0 | 26 | 20 |
| Lynch | 41.0 | 32 | 23 |
| Rice | 41.0 | 35 | 9 |
| Sapp | 40.0 | 33 | 7 |
| D. Smith | 38.0 | 35 | 3 |
| Wyms | 27.0 | 21 | 8 |
| Spires | 27.0 | 21 | 10 |
| Webster | 23.0 | 19 | 10 |
| Ivy | 22.0 | 21 | 0 |
| Darby | 21.0 | 16 | 6 |
| Howell | 21.0 | 19 | 2 |
| McFarland | 12.0 | 12 | 7 |
| Yoder | 9.0 | 8 | 3 |
| Phillips | 8.0 | 7 | 1 |
| Stecker | 8.0 | 7 | 1 |
| Nece | 8.0 | 7 | 2 |
| Golden | 7.0 | 6 | 2 |
| Gramatica | 3.0 | 3 | 0 |
| McCardell | 2.0 | 2 | 0 |
| Tupa | 2.0 | 1 | 0 |
| Pittman | 2.0 | 2 | 0 |
| Gurley | 2.0 | 2 | 0 |
| Crawford | 2.0 | 2 | 0 |
| Coleman | 2.0 | 2 | 0 |
| Claybrooks | 2.0 | 1 | 3 |
| Barnes | 2.0 | 2 | 0 |
| Alstott | 2.0 | 2 | 0 |
| K. Johnson | 1.0 | 1 | 0 |

| Player | No | Solo | Ast |
|---|---|---|---|
| Jenkins | 1.0 | 1 | 0 |
| Dilger | 1.0 | 1 | 0 |
| Walker | 1.0 | 1 | 0 |
| Cook | 1.0 | 1 | 0 |
| C. Smith | 1.0 | 1 | 0 |

## SACKS

| Player | No |
|---|---|
| Rice | 15.5 |
| Sapp | 7.5 |
| Wyms | 5.5 |
| Spires | 3.5 |
| Barber | 3 |
| Darby | 1.5 |
| McFarland | 1.5 |
| Brooks | 1 |
| Kelly | 1 |
| Quarles | 1 |
| Singleton | 1 |
| C. Smith | 1 |

## INTERCEPTIONS

| Player | No | Yds | Avg | TD |
|---|---|---|---|---|
| Kelly | 8 | 68 | 8 | 0 |
| Brooks | 5 | 218 | 43 | 3 |
| D. Smith | 4 | 39 | 9 | 0 |
| Lynch | 3 | 0 | 0 | 0 |
| Jackson | 3 | 101 | 33 | 0 |
| Sapp | 2 | 0 | 0 | 0 |
| Quarles | 2 | 29 | 14 | 1 |
| Barber | 2 | 9 | 4 | 0 |
| Rice | 1 | 30 | 30 | 0 |
| Singleton | 1 | 0 | 0 | 0 |

# TEAM

| | Buccaneers | Opp |
|---|---|---|
| Touchdowns | 35 | 21 |
| Rushing | 6 | 8 |
| Passing | 23 | 10 |
| Defensive | 5 | 3 |
| First downs | 287 | 236 |
| Rushing | 90 | 79 |
| Passing | 172 | 131 |
| Penalty | 25 | 26 |
| 3rd down: made/att | 79/222 | 75/223 |
| Net yards rushing | 1557 | 1554 |
| Net yards passing | 3445 | 2490 |

# Orlando Sentinel

OrlandoSentinel.com

The entire staff of the *Orlando Sentinel* contributed to the coverage of the Tampa Bay Buccaneers' amazing season. We gratefully acknowledge the efforts of the Photography and Sports Departments.

## SPORTS STAFF

Lynn Hoppes, Executive Sports Editor
Bill Speros, Deputy Sports Editor
Roger Simmons, Deputy Sports Editor
Mike Huguenin, Assistant Sports Editor/Football Editor
David Georgette, Assistant Sports Editor/Copy Chief
Dee Gugel, Assistant Sports Editor/High Schools
Chris Hays, Weekend Sports Editor
Joan Andrews, Sports Graphics Editor
Chris Rukan, Designer
Greg Hardy, Designer
Pam Dowd, Designer
Scott Andera, Copy Editor
Ken Gladstone, Copy Editor
Bruce Isphording, Copy Editor
LC Johnson, Copy Editor
Steve Ruiz, Copy Editor
Phil Tatman, Copy Editor
Lonnie Knabel, Graphic Artist
Mark Blythe, Clerk
David Marsters, Clerk
Tiffiney Symonette, Clerk

Mike Bianchi, Columnist
Jerry Greene, Columnist
David Whitley, Columnist
Bill Buchalter, Reporter
Jerry Brewer, Reporter
Frank Carroll, Reporter
Ryan Clark, Reporter
Buddy Collings, Reporter
George Diaz, Reporter
Steve Elling, Reporter
Chris Harry, Reporter
Ed Hinton, Reporter
Tim Povtak, Reporter
Josh Robbins, Reporter
Joe Schad, Reporter
Alan Schmadtke, Reporter
Brian Schmitz, Reporter
Shannon Shelton, Reporter
Joe Williams, Reporter
Don Wilson, Reporter
Lawrence Hollyfield, Contributor

## PHOTOGRAPHY STAFF

Tom Burton, Photo Editor
John Raoux, Photographer
Gary W. Green, Photographer
Shoun A. Hill, Photographer
Bobby Coker, Photographer
Ed Sackett, Photographer
George Skene, Photographer
Red Huber, Photographer
Steve Dowell, Photographer
Roberto Gonzalez, Photographer
Jessica Mann, Photographer

Hilda M. Perez, Photographer
Angela Peterson, Photographer
Joe Burbank, Photographer
Julie Fletcher, Photographer
Lee Fiedler, Photo Editor
Karen Jennings, Photo Technician
Jacob Langston, Photo Technician
Bradley Logan, Photo Technician
Larry Lopez, Photo Technician
Judith Padilla, Photo Technician